JU

A PLAIN VIEW OF THE CLAIMS OF THE ORTHODOX CATHOLIC CHURCH

AS OPPOSED TO ALL OTHER CHRISTIAN DENOMINATIONS

NIHIL SINE DEO

Author: **Julian Joseph Overbeck**
Editor: **Francesco Tosi**
Editio Princeps: *A plain view of the claims of the Orthodox Catholic Church as opposed to all other Christian Denominations, Trubner & Ludgate Hill, London, 1881.*

ISBN paperback: 9781650340227

A PLAIN VIEW OF THE CLAIMS

OF THE

ORTHODOX CATHOLIC CHURCH

AS OPPOSED TO ALL OTHER

CHRISTIAN DENOMINATIONS.

BY

J. J. OVERBECK, D.D.

"The Church of the living God,
the pillar and ground of the truth."
—1 TIM. iii. 15.

LONDON:
TRÜBNER & CO., LUDGATE HILL.

ST. PETERSBURG:
H. SCHMITZDORFF (K. RÖTTGER)
Kaiserl. Hofbuchhandlung.

LEIPZIG:
F. A. BROCKHAUS.
ATHENS: K. WILBERG.

CONSTANTINOPLE: S. H. WEISS, 481 GRANDE RUE DE PÉRA.
NEW YORK: E. STEIGER, 22 & 24 FRANKFORT STREET.

Two Shillings and Sixpence.

As the ORTHODOX CATHOLIC REVIEW is not intended to be a periodical of merely ephemeral interest, but proposes chiefly to contribute to the stock of Orthodox literature by Essays, Reviews, and Translations of a more lasting character, we venture to point out some of the papers which, at any time, might enlist the attention of the reader:

VOL. I.

Catholic Orthodoxy and Evangelicalism.
Russian Theological Literature.
"Ancient Roman Inscriptions."
"Christendom's Divisions."
Audiatur et altera pars.
The Real Presence and the Real Absence.
Our Position opposite Roman Catholicism.
Gordian Knots.
Greek Theological Literature.

VOL. II.

Orthodoxy, Anglicanism, and Romanism (Neale, Newman, Palmer, Allies).
Pope and Patriarch.
Rejection of the Council of Florence.
On the Relation of the Anglican Church to the Orthodox. By Professor DAMALAS. (Continued in Vols. III. and IV.)
The False Decretals.
Attempt at a Reunion of the Anglican and the Orthodox Church, made by the Non-Jurors.
Historical Witness against the Church of Rome and its Counterfeit.

VOL. III.

Reconsideration of the Anglican Claims. (Also to be had as pamphlet.)
The Liturgy of the Western Orthodox Catholic Mass.
The Succession of the Patriarchs of Constantinople.
The Hellenic College in London.
The Old-Catholic Movement and the Munich Congress.

VOL. IV.

The Bonn Conference.
Neologism and Orthodoxy.
The Great Canon of S. Andrew of Crete.
The only Safe Expedient for Roman Catholics. (Continued in Vol. V.)
Articles of Catholic and Orthodox Belief.
Confusion! Letters addressed to an Anglican Churchman. (Continued in Vols. V. and VI.)

[*Continued on page 3.*

A PLAIN VIEW OF THE CLAIMS

OF THE

ORTHODOX CATHOLIC CHURCH

AS OPPOSED TO ALL OTHER

CHRISTIAN DENOMINATIONS.

BY

J. J. OVERBECK, D.D.

"The Church of the living God,
the pillar and ground of the truth."
—1 TIM. iii. 15.

LONDON:
TRÜBNER & CO., LUDGATE HILL.
1881.

Ballantyne Press
BALLANTYNE, HANSON AND CO
EDINBURGH AND LONDON

CONTENTS.

A PLAIN VIEW OF THE CLAIMS

OF THE

ORTHODOX CATHOLIC CHURCH

AS APPOSED TO ALL OTHER CHRISTIAN DENOMINATIONS.

NO Christian denies that Christ founded One Church, and *only One.*

No Christian denies that this Church was to be *Catholic*, *i.e.*, universal, destined to embrace all mankind.

No Christian denies that this Church is *Holy*, offering the means of sanctification to the believer.

But here the agreement ends, for there are not a few Protestants who deny the fourth characteristic mark of Christ's Church, viz., that she must be *Apostolic.* They maintain that Paul preached not the same doctrine as Peter, and that both differed from John and James. In short, they maintain that already in the Apostolic times doctrinal corruption began to spread within the pale of the Church, and continued in her ever since, till the so-called Reformers set themselves to purify her, followed by their Rationalistic successors, sweeping away whatever of dust and cobwebs they still consider to hang about. Now, the individuality and temperament of the Apostles were, indeed, different, as there are not, never have been, and never will be, two persons exactly alike in their mode of thinking and of expressing their thoughts. Thus the Apostles, though holding the same truth, look at it from different points of view, as you may look at an object from different sides. So it was wisely arranged by God, in order to exhibit His truth in the most comprehensive way. Thus St. Paul shows the supreme value of *faith*, without, however, undervaluing *good works*, as the legitimate and necessary fruits of faith; while St. James lays a particular stress on "good works," so far as they spring from "faith," and prove that the faith producing them was not a mere sham, but a substantial reality. The depth of truth can never be *exhausted*, for it is conterminous with God, who is *the truth* (St. John xiv. 6). Our idea does not comprehend and encompass the fulness of any divine truth. It is the nature of a finite being that it cannot comprehend an infinite being, nor an infinite inexhaustible truth, or else the finite embracing the infinite would be greater than the latter, and consequently both change places—the individual would become God, and God would become the individual's creature. But what we mean to affirm is this, that the individual must be able to form a correct idea of the truth revealed by God for the benefit and guidance of man. There is a great difference between a *correct* idea and a *complete* idea. A correct idea of truth is indispensable to us for attaining our end; an incorrect idea is a wrong way that cannot lead to our destination. A *complete and exhaustive* idea of divine truth is impossible to man, since the finite capacity of man is not commensurate to the infinite comprehensiveness of divine thought. Thus the Apostles give us *different* (but by no means *conflicting*) aspects of the same truth—like the rays of the sun converging into the same centre—they are all *correct*, and tend towards *completing* the one unfathomable idea of divine conception (if we may transfer this human expression to divine intuition). Rationalism does not see this harmony of Apostolic teaching, because Rationalism is like a *prism*, the dispersive powers of which divide the ray of light, whereas Orthodoxy gathers the different rays of the one light and brings them back to its centre of unity. This Rationalism, the legitimate development of the fundamental Reformation principle, "the right of private judgment," has not only undermined the foundation of Christianity, but has scarcely left a shadow of the doctrine revealed by Christ. All miracles and prophecies are gone, *i.e.*, have dwindled away before the ever-increasing light of modern culture, which tried to prove them to be impositions, hypocrisies, or the fruit of blindness and ignorance. Christ, undeified, has been degraded to the rank of Solon, Pythagoras, Plato, and Confucius. His *Moral Code*, the only piece of property left to Him, is enthusiastically praised, as if to pacify and console Him for the deprivation of the rest. But even this "Moral Code" is antiquated, since it is based on *a clear and distinct notion of God* as revealed to Moses, to the Patriarchs, and Prophets. Rationalism cannot accept such a God, but can only admit a *hazy notion of the Deity*, leaving altogether aside the question whether God is a *Personality* or simply the *Vital Force* pervading Nature. Hence the doubts and misgivings about the creation of the world and the immortality of the soul.

This picture is not exaggerated, though all the Rationalists do not go the same length: yea, a great many of them would be frightened if they saw the abyss towards which they are hastening. But the constraint of logic is all but irresistible, and drags along those who once shuddered at a notion they now hold and stubbornly defend.

The Christian cloak and nomenclature is retained by the Rationalistic clergy for decency's sake, or as a bait for the ignorant and unsuspecting people. But, alas! the technical terms are empty; the Bible is nothing but a human work of literature, subject to the critical whims and conjectures of classical, historical, and physical scholars. The chief judge and ruler in the matter are the *Experimental Sciences.* Hence the depreciation of all *supernatural truth.* "We know only what our senses can perceive; all that is beyond this is mere supposition and guesswork." This is the main drift of Rationalistic argument, though it generally does not appear in this crude form, which would be too unpalatable to many who are first to be educated into a more advanced frame of Free Thought.

There are millions of Protestants belonging to this class of religionists. They do not form a separate denomination, but are content to remain where they hitherto were, in the Lutheran, or the Reformed, or the Presbyterian, or the Anglican, or any other Protestant Church. They are the solvent which inevitably must dissolve the Protestant Church, since it is not a heterogeneous matter inserted into the Protestant body, but the legitimate development of its own fundamental principle. The more far-sighted among the Unitarians declare openly that they prefer those who sympathise with them not to leave their present Church, but to serve as a leaven slowly penetrating the mass. And, indeed, is the *fashionable* Christianity of the present day, the Christianity of the leading actors, authors, artists, anything else but what we have just described? How utterly Christianity has disappeared from this sort of religion is evident from the fact that the modern school of Reform-Jews advocate the amalgamation with the Unitarians and their co-religionists scattered about in the different Protestant Churches. Marriages between Jews and Christians are no longer called *scandals*, but clergymen are found to officiate and call down God's blessing on such unions, and persons of the most exalted rank of society honour the ceremony with their presence. These are signs of the times more eloquent than a thousand arguments, and pointing in this direction: that the Protestant Church is drifting into *unbelief*, which is next-door neighbour to *infidelity*. And, what is the worst, it is just the consistent and rigorous development of the fundamental Protestant principle of private judgment which *leads naturally and inevitably* to unbelief.

It is only by *inconsistency* and *self-delusion* that a Protestant can be a believer. If he refrains from drawing the necessary conclusions from his premisses, because his better self warns him and his religious feeling is revolted at the logical result, he ought to examine his principle and reject it, instead of proclaiming it yet not following it up to the bitter end. This is *glaring inconsistency*. If, moreover, this private judgment breeds an infinity of different opinions on the same doctrine, common sense tells us that, at best, only one can be right, and the others are misleading. But where is the tribunal to decide who is right and who is wrong? It is a cheap and flimsy excuse to maintain that the pious Christians agree in all fundamental doctrines. History tells us just the contrary, and only he who *will* be blind can advance such a view. However, let us, only for argument's sake, grant the assertion: who is to decide which doctrines ought to be considered fundamental? The pious Protestant Claus Harms tells us that you can write the doctrines in which the Protestants agree on the nail of your finger. Such has become Christ's doctrine under the management of private judgment.

"*The Bible, the Bible only, and nothing but the Bible*," is the symbol and device of the believing Protestant. It is nothing but *self-delusion* which prompts him to profess this tenet. For from whom did he receive the Bible, and who vouches for its authenticity and integrity? Biblical research and criticism have at least had the good consequence to open the eyes of those blind people who believed that the Bible, ready made, had fallen from heaven, every letter miraculously written by God's own finger. And the translation? Was this perhaps also God's infallible work? And what is the recently revised translation? If anything brings discredit on Protestantism, it is this unreasonable worship of the Bible, this *Bibliolatria.* The Bible is essentially a *Church-book.* The Holy Ghost intrusted it to the Church. The Church has kept and keeps it undefiled. The Church knows its origin, and vouches for its authenticity and integrity. The Church gives it to her children and explains its meaning. The Church makes it, by her infallible guidance, the richest source of blessings to her children. But the Bible, purloined and snatched from the hands of the Church, is apt to become a curse to those whom it was to benefit, and has been made the fruitful mother of heresies, of follies, and vagaries. If the Protestants, nevertheless, find many Church doctrines in the Bible, they simply, though perhaps unconsciously, borrowed them from the Church and interpreted them into the Bible, and consequently found them in the same. The Protestants are ignorant of how much the traditions of the Church influenced their understanding of the Bible. It is not "*the Bible only*" which guides them, but

Tradition; yet they persuade themselves that it is the Bible, and not Tradition. This is the Protestant's *self-delusion.*

Though we naturally must find fault with this inconsistency and self-delusion of the believing Protestant, yet we consider them a blessing for those poor souls who thus have preserved some treasures of the Church, whereas otherwise they would have fallen into unbelief.

Now, to return to the exposition in the beginning of this paper. The believing Protestant recognises the fourth characteristic mark of the Church, viz., her *Apostolicity.* But what are we to understand by this word? "Of course," the reader will say, "the Apostolic doctrine on which the Church is built." But here the Irvingites step forward, protesting against such a misunderstanding, since "it is real and live Apostles we need, and not only their doctrine." They base their claims on Ephes. iv. 11–13 and 1 Cor. xii. 28; and why should they not? As genuine Protestants, they stick to the *letter* of the Bible, without taking any notice of how the Church understood the passages quoted, and the *letter* was decidedly on their side. But why did, then, not the bulk of Protestants follow (or rather precede) them in advocating an "Apostolic" ministry? No doubt the latent cause was chiefly the silent and unconscious influence of the Church's traditional interpretation. But, besides, the "Apostolic" theory was beset with so many practical difficulties, that men of a sober mind directly saw its utter impracticability. After the first twelve, chosen by Christ Himself, and St. Matthias and St. Paul, appointed by Divine revelation, and recognised as such by their colleagues, there never had been in the Church an Apostle nor a demand for them. How to get them now? As "Apostles are neither of men nor by man, but by Jesus Christ and God the Father, sent forth immediately and directly" (as the Irvingite Catechism has it), how could anybody pretending to have a Divine call as Apostle offer any credentials? Were we simply to believe his word, or was his claim to be confirmed by miracles and prophecies? We do not know of any miracles wrought by Irvingite Apostles. And as to the numerous Irvingite prophecies, they have proved exceedingly unfortunate. But did not the "Prophets" testify to the Divine call of the new Apostles? Indeed! But how did the Prophets prove their own call and mission? Here we are at a dead-lock, and the claims of the Apostles, however unimpeachable and even saintly their characters may be, collapse before reason and common sense. Yet this condemnation becomes stronger still when we see that this modern Apostle is essentially different from the primitive one. The Irvingite Apostles do not go out preaching the Gospel and teaching all nations; they do not affect personal *infallibility* in their teaching (as the primitive Apostles possessed it), nor *inspiration* in their Epistles and Encyclicals. They prudently avoided, by curtailing their own claims, the responsibility for errors and inconsistencies; but they overlooked that, by so doing, they created an entirely new system of Apostleship, a novelty unheard of in the Christian Church before 1830.

But the wise inconsistency of the Irvingites in limiting the rights and endowments of their Apostles was not adopted by the only other Protestant denomination which claims to possess Apostles, viz., the *Mormons*. This sect, considerably more numerous but less respectable than the former, equally sprang up in 1830. They are, indeed, consistent with a vengeance! Their Holy Scriptures comprise not only the Bible, the Book of Mormon, the Revelations contained in the collection entitled "The Pearl of Great Price," but all other Apostolic revelations and injunctions, past, present, and future. The frame and filling-in of their Church fabric is richer and more comprehensive than that of any other Church. Not content with one priesthood, they have two—the Aaronic and the Melchisedekian. Not content with introducing Spiritism into their theological system, they add to it our modern Materialism. Their God is a palpable and measurable being, and every one of the faithful is to become a God. Matter is eternal, and God is Matter.

Consistency of error leads most certainly to its self-destruction. Thus we see Mormonism landing on the shore of Materialism, which is identical with Atheism—as we see likewise Buddhism, that Pagan mirage of a Christian High Church, sunk in the Nirvana of Atheism.

After having disposed of the modern Apostles and thus cleared our way, we may, without contradiction on the part of the remaining believing Christians, affirm that Christ's Church is called *Apostolic*, because she descends in an unbroken line from the Apostles, and professes the doctrines taught by the Apostles, neither adding to nor subtracting from them.

Thus far the four characteristic marks of Christ's Church are settled. Now the more difficult task remains to show what we are to understand by the word CHURCH.

Considering the word *Church* or *Kirk* from an etymological point of view, we find that all Teutonic, Scandinavian, and Slavonic languages (with the solitary exception of the Polish *kościoł*) derive the word from the Greek *kyriake* (*κυριακὴ* sc. *οἰκία*), "the house of the Lord." Originally it signified the building erected for the meeting of the faithful, but it soon got the secondary meaning of "the household of the Lord" assembled in the building. The word, though Greek, is not used by the Greek Church in this meaning, but the Greek, Latin, Romance, Welsh, and Armenian languages use the word *ecclesia* (*ἐκκλησία*), which means "an assembly convoked by authority."

Thus we see that throughout the range occupied by the Aryan or Indo-European languages the notion of "the Church" is specified by two cognate and most expressive ideas, supplementing and completing each other, viz., *kyriake*, "the household of God's and Christ's people," and *ecclesia*, "the congregation convoked by the authority of Christ and of those to whom He gave authority."

It is most remarkable that in the domain of the Semitic languages, more particularly in Hebrew and Syro-Chaldaic (the language spoken by our Saviour), the same bifurcation of expressions exists: (1.) The Hebrew *qahal* (קָהָל, coetus, congregatio) is derived from a root which is identical with the Greek *καλέω*, the Dutch *kallen*, and the English *to call*, and signifies "a congregation called together," implying influence or authority able to make the call effective. Deut. xxxi. 30 the LXX. translates this word by *ἐκκλησία*, agreeably to our above explanation. (2.) The Hebrew *édah* (עֵדָה) and Syro-

Chaldaic *idta* (עִדְתָא) signify a congregation convened at a fixed spot; hence a congregation bound together by certain bonds. Therefore (Job xvi. 7 and xv. 34) it is used in the meaning of *family* or *household*, like the secondary meaning of *kyriake*. The Syriac Peshito (of the second century), and Cureton's still older version of the Gospel of St. Matthew, use constantly the term *idta* for "Church," and there is no doubt that this was the very word used by our Saviour.

The result of this etymological inquiry is, that the notion of the word *Church* includes the two ideas: (1) that she is a congregation called together and kept together *by authority;* (2) that she is the *household of God* and *Christ's family.*

Christianity is a *historical product*, and not simply a *philosophical system.* Hence the uppermost importance of *Tradition*, which, properly understood, is only another name for *History.* It is simply an abuse of our language to interpret the word "Tradition" by "nursery tales," "superstitious legends," "fond things vainly invented." Thus our Historical or Traditional Christianity sprang from incontestable facts, far beyond the reach and beyond the cavil of our fashionable critics. If we will be Christians, we must take Christianity as a *hard and stubborn fact*, such as History, uncorrupted History, has handed it down to us, and not as a *soft, workable, and kneadable dough*, from which the skilful hand of the workman or modeller can shape any fancy of his brain. To thousands of Christians the Bible is this shapeless mass, from which they form their different and multitudinous castles in the air, dubbing them "the Church of Christ." A little common sense must show to any sound mind how utterly futile these pretensions are; and certainly there would not be such a cloud of pretenders claiming to possess "Christ's true Church," had not Protestantism taught them the specious phrase "*to think for themselves*," *i.e.*, to act independently and shun the trammels of *Authority.*

Now, the Historical Church of Christ is an institution clothed by Christ with authority, as we saw above. Christ's words in this respect are most explicit and unmistakable: "If he neglect to hear the Church, let him be unto thee as an heathen man and a publican" (St. Matt. xviii. 17). The objection raised here, that Jesus does not refer to the Christian but to the Jewish Church, is of no avail, for our Orthodox Church always and emphatically declared that she only knows and recognises *One Church*, founded in Paradise, when the first promise of the Saviour was proclaimed, and reaching into eternity. This *continuous* Church naturally fell into the *Church of promise* and the *Church of fulfilment*, both guided by the same Holy Ghost, both essentially Christian, either prospectively or retrospectively.

Thus the Church's *authority* cannot be doubted. But who is vested with this authority? Is the Church an *absolute democracy*, so that every member has a vote in all Church matters, and the Holy Ghost guiding the Church *has to yield to majorities, public opinion, and intrigues?* Common sense tells us that such cannot be the case, and the experience of hundreds of Christian sects contradicting and annihilating each other corroborates the conclusion we arrive at, that there must be a *board of authorities* in the Church, to whom we are bound to submit. This is also the express teaching of Christ. He says (St. Matt. xxiii. 2, 3), "The Scribes and the Pharisees sit in Moses' seat: all therefore whatsoever they bid you observe, that observe and do; but do not ye after their works." Dr. Warburton correctly explains this passage: "Our Lord instructs His hearers . . . that ministers of religion, who sit in Moses' chair, and are *invested with authority to teach the law*, are to be attended to as instructors when in their office they announce and enforce the ordinances of God."

We shall see presently who were the legitimate successors of the Scribes and Pharisees in the New Testament dispensation. But let us first consider the concluding words of the above passage: " . . . but do not ye after their works." These words disclose a most important characteristic mark of the Church, viz., its *visibility*. If a bad Churchman, in consequence of his wickedness, would cease to be a real member of the Church, how could bad Church authorities retain their power in the sight of God, and justly claim our obedience? Yet this is the case, as Christ teaches us. Christ knows *withered* branches in the vine (a symbol of the mystical body of the Church), yet they remain (though lifeless, *i.e.*, deprived of the life of grace) in the vine till they are cut off (*i.e.*, excommunicated). Here we see the glaring heresy of Huss, Wycliffe, and the great majority of believing Protestants, who declare the real Church of Christ to be *the invisible Church of the elect*, and not the visible body of professing Christians, composed of good and bad ones.

It is astonishing how deep-seated this Protestant principle of the all-sufficiency of an Invisible Church is even in many Anglicans who are standing on the threshold of the Orthodox Church. They argue: "If I only hold all the truths of the Orthodox Church, it matters little whether I join it outwardly." They do not see that by so speaking they betray that they do not hold all the Orthodox truths, since they deny the visibility of the Church by denying *the duty and necessity* of joining the visible Orthodox Church.

A consequence of the Invisible Church theory is the predominant belief among Protestants that all the different Christian denominations constitute the One Church of Christ. They are expected to sink their vital differences and to unite on common ground. But there is the difficulty. Who would be willing to give up what he considers vital? And which is the common ground? The "Evangelical Alliance" tried the experiment with a set of kindred Protestant sects, and has so far succeeded that it spread a levelling indifference.

However, it would be time and labour lost if we tried to refute a theory so utterly opposed to Christ's teaching: "Go ye, therefore, and teach all nations, baptizing them, ... teaching them to observe ALL THINGS WHATSOEVER I HAVE COMMANDED YOU: and, lo, I am with you alway, even unto the end of the world. Amen" (St. Matt. xxviii. 19, 20). From this passage we see—

1. That not a *selection* of doctrines is sufficient, but that *all things whatsoever* Christ has commanded His Apostles are requisite and necessary, and that the want or misconstruction of one single doctrine frustrates all Church claims.

2. That Christ refers us to the *living voice* of the Church, *i.e.*, to the Apostles and their lawful successors, whom He charged with teaching all nations, and with whom He promised to be "*alway*, even unto the end of the world," assisting, enlightening, guiding into all truth. That this charge and assistance was not to be confined to the Apostles, but extended to their lawful successors, we know from the Apostles, who actually appointed their successors, the Bishops. Moreover, Christ's promise to be *alway* with them, *even unto the end of the world*, implied the successors of the Apostles, or else would have been unmeaning.

3. That the Bible was not given us as our *guide, standard, and rule of faith.* This was simply impossible, since not a word of the New Testament was written down before the year 52, when the First Epistle to the Thessalonians was issued. The first Gospel was not published until after the year 66, and the last books of the New Testament were written about the end of the first century. And when could possibly the whole of the New Testament have become known to all the Churches? Moreover, most of the Epistles were occasional writings, addressed to local Churches, or to certain disciples of the Apostles. Again, the Church was not in a hurry in drawing up a Canon of the inspired books of the New Testament, for up to the fourth century the "Revelation" of St. John was not generally recognised.* What do the Bible-Christians say to this? Many flourishing Churches existed in the East and West, yet there was no Bible! Whence was the doctrine and practice of these Churches derived? FROM THE ORAL TEACHING OF THE APOSTLES. Those Christians knew, without the Bible, their Catechism as well as we do.†

---

* The Canon does not even contain all the inspired books of the New Testament, for we see from 1 Cor. v. 9 *seq.* that what we now call the First Epistle to the Corinthians was preceded by another Epistle to the same Church. It is merely a gratuitous assumption when the Anglican Bishop Tomline suggests "that St. Paul referred to the former part" of our present First Corinthians. It is apparently the sore perplexity of a Protestant being obliged to admit that the New Testament does not contain all the inspired books that made him advance such an untenable suggestion. And St. Paul's Epistle to the Laodiceans (Col. iv. 16), where is it? It was not identical with that to the Ephesians (as some suppose), but a separate Epistle, as Dr. Adalbert Maier (*Einleitung in die Schriften des Neuen Testaments*, p. 310) and Dr. J. Langen have fully shown. Thus *both these Epistles have been entirely lost.*

† Even the Anglo-American Bishop Dr. A. N. Littlejohn, though a Protestant,

And when at last the New Testament in its entirety appeared, it was only a summary of the Church doctrine, or rather *the written part of Church Tradition;* for it appears nowhere in the New Testament that the Written Word is to supersede the Tradition, but St. Paul most explicitly enjoins, "Therefore, brethren, stand fast, and hold the Traditions which ye have been taught, whether by word or our epistle" (2 Thess. ii. 15). And St. Irenæus (a disciple of St. Polycarp, who was himself a disciple of the Apostle St. John) writes thus: "We ought not to seek among others the truth, which we may have for asking from the Church. For in her, as in a rich treasure-house, *the Apostles have laid up in its fulness all that pertains to the truth*, so that whosoever seeketh may receive from her the food of life. She is the door of life" (Adv. Hæres. iii. 4). Such is the truth which the Apostle St. John taught St. Polycarp, and St. Polycarp* taught St. Irenæus, and St. Irenæus together with the whole Orthodox Church teaches us. Very different is the teaching of Luther and Calvin, Zwingli and Cranmer. They built the Bible on the ruins of the Church (we do not mean the corrupted Roman Church, but the undefiled Church of undivided Christendom, the Church of the Seven Œcumenical Councils). The so-called Reformers snatched the Bible from the Church, its divinely instituted keeper and possessor, and delivered it up to the private judgment of the people, but soon found out that by appropriating the Bible they had lost the key to its meaning, which key was left in the possession of the Church. The Orthodox Church never at any time forbade the reading of the Bible—as the Roman Church did—but, on the contrary, encouraged its reading, provided the

---

agrees with us. In his sermons on *Individualism*, preached before the University of Cambridge in November 1880 (Cambridge: Deighton, Bell, & Co.) he says: "There is a vague and unreasoning notion that Christianity was taken from the New Testament. The notion is historically untrue; Christianity was widely extended through the civilised world before the New Testament was written; and its several books were successively addressed to various bodies of Christian believers —to bodies, that is, who already possessed the faith of Christ in its *integrity*. . . . Christianity is not taken from it (the New Testament); for it existed before it."

* St. Polycarp "departed this life, having always taught the things which he had learnt from the Apostles, and which the Church has handed down, and *which alone are true*" (St. Iren. contra Hær., iii. 3, 4).

reader sought its meaning from the Church, and did not follow his own imagination.

Of course the Protestants produce some Bible passages in which they think to find their estimate of the Bible as the only source of Divine doctrine. The chief passage is St. John v. 39 : " Search the Scriptures." This, however, refers to the Old Testament, not as a proof of its containing all the doctrines of the Jewish Church, but as " testifying of the Messiah." Still, this very passage implies a condemnation of the Protestant Bible-reading, for Jesus adds to the words, " Search the Scriptures " the significant words, " for in them ye think ye have eternal life "—(but you have not, because you twist the words according to your private judgment, and thus obscure and misinterpret the Messianic prophecies). These words in brackets are the natural completion of the sentence.

Most Protestants take St. John v. 39 as a solemn injunction of our Saviour, addressed to all the faithful, to read the Bible. But whoever reads carefully St. John v. 39 will easily see that the meaning is not a *command* but a *hypothesis*, equivalent to " If you read the Scriptures, you will find that they testify of Me." But the translation, " Search the Scriptures " is not so certain as people think, for the Greek original can also be translated, " *Ye search* the Scriptures." And this apparently fits better into the context. Therefore the new revision of the English authentic version, following in the wake of the best and most reliable scholars and translators of our time, has adopted it.

The futility of the Protestant Bible claims is obvious if we go back from the nineteenth century to the times of Jesus and the Apostles. Bible-readers are too apt to think that every Jew had a copy of the Bible, such as the Bible Society disseminates broadcast; that every Jew, in the morning and evening, called together his household to read a chapter of the Bible, as a genuine Protestant does. Now this is all fancy. At the time of Jesus and the Apostles the Temple and the Synagogues possessed copies of the Pentateuch, the Prophets, and the Psalms, perhaps also of most of the Hagiographa (for the Song of Songs, Ecclesiastes, and Esther were not yet generally recognised). But it is more than doubtful whether one in ten thousand Jews possessed a copy even of the five books of Moses. Not every one could afford the expense of having them copied. But it was not necessary, for the Jewish Church read and explained all the most important parts of the Bible throughout the year. The child had to learn by heart (as it is still the custom with the stricter class of the Jews) the Psalms and portions of the Pentateuch. The Prophets were constantly read and exhaustively treated, as we know from Jesus's visit to the Temple. In short, *the Church was the only dispenser and interpreter of the Bible*, and the Jewish Church did for her doctrine no more depend on the completion of her Canon than the Christian Church did on the completion of hers. Thus neither the Jews had, at the time of Jesus, what we would now call a complete Old Testament, nor had the Christians at the end of the first century what we would now call a complete New Testament; but the Church doctrine was known and taught all the same.

The pretended duty and necessity of private Bible-reading could never have been invented if another invention had not preceded it, viz., the art of printing; and we may safely call Bible-Christianity a legacy of Gutenberg and an offshoot of typography. The printed Bibles superseded Church-teaching.

It is an incontestable fact that the art of printing did not prove an unmixed boon. At the side of the comparatively few really good and useful books a deluge of trash and filth is hourly issuing from the printing press, inundating the world at large, spreading lies, exciting passions, inviting to sins and crimes, undermining religion, disturbing family, and poisoning society. We know the fanatic Bible-Christian will reply to this: "Whatever mischief bad literature may cause, the enormous spread of the Word of God will richly outweigh it." We are not so sure of this. First of all, is *your* Bible the Word of God? It is only a translation, a translation made by *uninspired* men—men who held sectarian views, and foisted their erroneous teachings into the Bible, palming them off as the Word of God—men who had only a superficial knowledge of the original languages, and, in consequence of it, introduced translations of passages of which there is not the remotest idea to be found in the text (*e.g.*, Luther's translation of Isaiah xxviii. 19). But let us turn to the original text. Where is it? It is more than doubtful whether we ever shall get the correct original text. The stupendous critical labours show that we only can hope to approach to a relatively pure text. Absolute purity is altogether out of the question. In the Old Testament we have adopted the Masorethic text, though the Greek translation of the LXX, used by the Greek Church, is very different, and the various readings, collected by Benjamin Kennikott, Bernard de Rossi, Abraham Geiger, &c., are truly crushing. As to the New Testament, the uncertainty of the text is almost equally great. The Vatican, Alexandrian, and Sinaitic Codices, and a great many others, used by Cardinal Ximenes, Erasmus, Beza, Brian Walton, Bengel, Griesbach, Lachmann, Scholz, Tischendorf, in their respective editions, offer such a multitude of various readings, that it is and ever will be simply impossible to evolve from them the undoubted original text. *Thus are we for ever to remain without the authentic text of the Old and New Testament?* Yes, it seems that God's Providence has ordered it so, and very wisely ordered it so. Had God wished us to possess the authentic text of the Bible, it would have been an easy thing to Him to preserve the original writings. But did it never strike you as a most curious and astonishing fact, that none of all the original sacred writings have been found, but only copies? Yet we possess undoubted originals of profane literature, hieroglyphic and cuneiform, reaching back as far as Moses. Thus, humanly speaking, we may, yea, we cannot but suppose that there was a certain *design* of God in allowing the sacred originals to be lost. And this design was no doubt God's will *that the Church should be the authoritative exponent of His doctrine and commandments.* God willed not to set His seal on the dead letter of a Book, which might tend to dispossessing His Church, which He charged—and her alone—with teaching all nations. Experience shows how wisely God has acted in withholding from the Bible that degree of certainty which originals would have offered. Now a Bible-Christian must be either an ignorant and unthinking man, or the history of the Bible and its text must lead him back to the Church and her teaching. We are prepared to hear the objection, "Has your Church, then, a better Bible to offer us than we possess already?" No, indeed, we have not; but what we have is *Christ's true doctrine bequeathed by Him to His Church, and preserved by the continual assistance and guidance of the Holy Ghost.* Thus the Bible in possession of the Church is a fountain of life, and does not give currency to doctrinal errors or adulterate the meaning of the words of the Apostles, because it was just the oral teaching of the Apostles which constitutes the doctrine of the Church, and has constituted it before a single word of the New Testament was written down. Whatever improvements critical scholars will introduce into the text of the Bible, we thankfully accept them, since we know that any sound critical improvement can only be in accordance with the Church's doctrine; for the Holy Ghost, both guiding the Church and inspiring the authors of the Holy Scriptures, cannot contradict Himself. Even where the Bible-Christian is startled and despondingly shakes his head when he sees the pruning-knife of sound criticism cutting away favourite props and evidences of his belief (*e.g.*, 1 John v. 7), the Orthodox is perfectly quiet and unshaken, for his belief does not depend on a passage of the Bible, but on the teaching of the Church. The wording of any Biblical passage depends, with us, on full and sound critical evidence, and this evidence is against the second half of the 7th verse of 1 John v., which is manifestly an interpolation, as even the Jesuit Peronne in his *Prælectiones Theologicæ* admits.

Thus we saw that the spread of the printed Bible is by no means an unmixed boon. However, we must go farther. The promiscuous and general use of the Bible is attended by *immense evils.* It is shocking to see a child handling the Bible and reading passages which a grown-up and married person blushes to read. Thus the poison of impurity is infused into the souls of the innocent. Those Bible-Christians cry out against the book "The Priest in Absolution," a book destined only for the guidance of priests, but they are not revolted at their own hypocrisy in placing in the hands of innocent children a book disclosing things more horrible than the book mentioned contains. Göthe in his "*Bekenntnisse einer schönen Seele*" refers to the words of a lady confessing that she had learnt more of what defiles the purity of the soul from the Bible than from any other book. In Holland exists the custom that in the morning and evening the household comes together, parents, children, and servants, to assist at the reading of the Bible, which is read through from beginning to end in the course of the year. Not a word is left out. Is this not a horrible profanation of God's Word? The Bible was not written for children and inexperienced persons, but for the Church to dispense from it to her children the food they need, wholesome and salutary food, not indigestible stuff or deadly poison. The Church, both the Jewish and the Christian, was most considerate and delicate in what it offered her children from the Bible. Thus Rabbi Nathan, Origen, and St. Jerome tell us that the Jews were forbidden to read "*the Song of Songs*" before they had attained their thirtieth year. And the Christians followed in this respect the Jews. The Church acted as a loving mother acts towards her children.

The Protestants, in making the Bible their one and all, were naturally led to suppose its *all-sufficiency* and *clearness.* But both these qualities are not only indemonstrable, but the very reverse can be shown by the clearest passages. If the Church existed a hundred years before the whole of the New Testament was written, and four hundred years before all its parts were generally recognised, the Protestant is bound to show the deed of superannuation by which the Church surrendered her authority to the Bible. Where is it to be found? Nowhere. And as to the *clearness* of the Bible, only children, old women, and infatuated fanatics can believe in it. If St. Peter found the Epistles of St. Paul difficult to understand, the divines of our days will scarcely dare to maintain that they understand them better than St. Peter did. And the Old Testament, with its thousand almost insurmountable difficulties, who can call it clear? Only ignorance or self-conceit can hazard such an assertion. There is such an utter want of common sense underlying the Protestant system, that it is scarcely credible that so many millions have yielded to it. However the real reason is this: if the Bible is man's sole authority, man—who is the sole interpreter of the Bible—is *his own authority.* Certainly nothing is more pleasing and acceptable to fallen mankind. Hence the enormous success of Protestantism.

Christ's Church was not a "Scripture Club" or "Theological Debating Society," but an institution vested with *authority*, doctrinal, sacramental, and disciplinary authority. This authority was exercised by the Apostles and their lawful successors, the Bishops. This we learn from the Bible and Tradition. The Apostles, when scattered abroad preaching the Gospel to all nations, were of necessity preserved from error, as otherwise the unity of the Church would have been defeated by the human diversity of teaching. But when they could consult together, the Holy Ghost guided infallibly their deliberations. When the Apostles had departed this life and deposited all the teaching of Christ in the Churches they founded, personal infallibility was no longer needed, and the Bishops had, in cases of controversy, to consult together, as the Apostles had set them an example in the first Council of Jerusalem. As the Apostles were of equal rank, so were and are the Bishops. Certain Apostles might have had a personal pre-eminence in some way, *e.g.*, St. Peter through his fervent faith, St. Paul through his wonderful activity, St. John through his love; yet all were officially of the same rank, had the same power and authority.

This equality of rank is stoutly denied by the Roman Church, which claims for Peter the Primacy among the Apostles; not an *honorary* Primacy, but a *real and distinctive* Primacy, *i.e.*, *Supremacy*. This claim is chiefly based on St. Matt. xvi. 18: "Thou art Peter, and upon this rock I will build my Church, and the gates of Hades shall not prevail against her." All depends on the meaning which the Church attaches to the word *Rock*. A genuine Catholic consults the Apostolic Tradition, as found in the Fathers of the Church. If the Fathers agree in their verdict, their voice is apparently the voice of the Church. But if it does not agree, the voice of the Fathers is only their personal and subjective opinion, and not the voice of the Church, and *can never become such.* Now, the French divine Launoy has taken the trouble to count the voices of the Fathers on this point, and finds that forty-four explain the "Rock" as "the belief in Christ's divinity," just confessed by Peter, or as "the person of Christ;" and only seventeen understand it of the person of Peter. Thus we are at liberty to explain the passage as we like. But however we may explain it, *we are not warranted to make a dogma of our subjective interpretation.* Every sincere Roman, who knows the first principles of the Catholic religion, must bend to these facts. But how the poor Romans are deceived and led astray by *impertinent and unblushing liars,* we see from Dr. Allioli's German Bible translation, approved by Pope Gregory XVI. The translator gives in a footnote the usual Roman interpretation, and adds: "So teach *all* the Holy Fathers" (!!!)

The Romans derive also Peter's claim to the Primacy from St. Luke xxii. 31, 32: "And the Lord said, Simon, Simon, behold, Satan hath desired to have you, that he may sift you as wheat: but I have prayed for thee, that thy faith fail not: and when thou art converted, strengthen thy brethren." The Holy Fathers generally understand this passage of the *grace of perseverance,* and refer it to all the faithful. Pope Honorius I., in his letter to the Archbishop of Canterbury, refers it to all the pastors of the Church. Those who refer it to Peter's Primacy do not go beyond the person of Peter, and do not apply it to his successors. Even the strongest language of Pope Agatho shows that he considers the range of Papal authority confined to the preservation of the decrees of the Œcumenical Councils. Thus, also this passage is, from a traditional point of view, *not conclusive.*

The third and last passage adduced as proof of Peter's Primacy is St. John xxi. 15–17. The feeding of Christ's lambs and sheep, intrusted by Him to Peter, is differently understood by the Holy Fathers. Some understand it of Peter's Primacy, others of the power given to the Apostles, whose representative was Peter. The latter (particularly St. Basil and St. Cyril of Alexandria) are most explicit in this respect. St. Basil winds up his argument by the significant words: "To all the following pastors and teachers He gives *the same power*." St. Cyril thinks that the thrice-repeated question of Christ refers to the thrice-repeated denial of Peter, and that the charge of feeding Christ's lambs and sheep was, as it were, a renewal of the Apostolate and a wiping away of the ignominy entailed by Peter's denial. To this second class of interpreters belongs, in the first place, St. Peter himself, who in his first Epistle, v. 1–3, plainly refers to our passage and claims no other dignity than that to be the *co-presbyter* (*συμπρεσβύτερος*) of those presbyters to whom he addresses his Epistles. It is a most telling fact that in the Epistles of St. Peter, where we should naturally look for some trace of the Apostle's "supreme authority," not the slightest hint can be discovered. If Peter had been "the visible head of the Church," he ought to have officially proclaimed such a prerogative. But he has not. This cannot be explained (as the Romans do) on the plea of St. Peter's humility, for it would have been false humility, abdication or undue concealment of his authoritative position. However, not only Peter's silence, but also clear facts show that Peter never dreamt of claiming a power and authority such as the Papists attribute to him. Gal. ii. 11–14 we read: "When Peter was come to Antioch, I resisted him to the face, because *he stood condemned* (*κατεγνωσμένος ἦν*). For before that certain came from James, he did eat with the Gentiles: but when they came, he drew back and separated himself, *fearing* them that were of the circumcision. *And the rest of the Jews dissembled likewise with him;* insomuch *that even Barnabas was carried with their dissimulation.* But when I saw that *they walked not uprightly according to the truth of the Gospel,* I said unto Peter before them all," &c. Was this act of human fear apt to realise the Lord's words, "Strengthen thy brethren"? Was it not leading astray the lambs and sheep intrusted to His care, so that *they dissembled likewise with him?* Is he the Rock upon which the Church is built who *walks not uprightly according to the truth of the Gospel?* And this "truth of the Gospel," which Peter *practically denied*, and by his example *caused others to deny*, was just the solemn decree moved and defended by Peter and unanimously accepted by the Council of the Apostles as the dictation of the Holy Ghost (Acts xv. 28)! And before this, Peter had been informed by a vision that the Gentiles were not unclean. Are these not aggravating circumstances, not very promising for the *prototype of Papal Infallibility?* The Romans like to skip over the above passage with an easy heart; St. Paul, St. Jerome, St. Augustine did not. And St. Hilary of Poitiers deduces from it the *equality in rank* of Peter and Paul: "Who would dare to resist St. Peter, a chief Apostle, unless it were another like him, who, confident of his own election, and knowing himself to be not unequal to him, could firmly disapprove of what the former had imprudently done?"

Another indisputable fact showing the groundlessness of the Roman view of St. Peter's authority is that he never exercised any acts of supremacy over the rest of the Apostles; *on the contrary, when* SENT BY THEM, *he obeyed* (Acts viii. 14). Here we see that the Council of the Apostles is a higher instance than the authority of any single apostle, Peter included. Therefore the Œcumenical Council is the highest instance in the Orthodox Catholic Church, to which Popes, Patriarchs, Bishops, and all the faithful have to submit.

The result of the preceding inquiry is, that the interpretation of none of the three passages on which the Romans base the claims of St. Peter to the supremacy in the Church is borne out by the *unanimis consensus* of the Fathers, consequently is not binding on us. If we were Protestants, whose doctrines stand or fall by Bible proof, we could here dismiss the question. But as our Church is based on the oral teaching of the Apostles, transmitted by Tradition, we are bound to ask, What does the Church say concerning St. Peter's Primacy? Here we find, indeed, the overwhelming majority of the Fathers constituting a moral *consensus* in favour of Peter's Primacy, and the Eastern Fathers are almost more eloquent in this respect than the Western.

But what are we to understand by *Primacy?* Is it simply the *Presidency* (*προεδρεία*) in the College of the Apostles, so that the President is only *primus inter pares?* Or is it the *Supremacy*, ruling over the other Apostles as *subjects?* The former view is taken by the Orthodox, the latter by the Romans.

If the reader opens a Roman book on the Papal claims, he will be terrified by the tremendous array of quotations from the Fathers in support of the Roman view. But let him not be alarmed. A few precautions will clear his way. (1.) Let him not trust any quotation before he has satisfied himself that the text is neither incomplete, truncated, interpolated, or spurious; (2.) That the text is correctly translated; (3.) That the passage is not a *subjective and merely personal opinion*, which has no value for supporting a doctrine—this rule will remove at least nine out of ten quotations; (4.) Only the passages claiming *the authority of tradition* are to be considered, and even in these we must not forget that the Fathers were fallible men; consequently, (5.) Only the *consensus* of the Fathers can decide. In this way our adversary's army will wonderfully shrink together.

Another point must be added, generally overlooked by the Romans. The Fathers are naturally infinitely more trustworthy when they state what the Church rejects as a heresy than when they describe a doctrine, for then, as a rule, they specify the Church's traditional teaching and not their private opinion, and we can suppose that they knew how to distinguish between truth and error. But in describing a doctrine they not unfrequently admix their personal speculation, evolving the doctrine from a theological or philosophical system, or supporting the doctrine by the system. In this respect the Fathers of the Alexandrian school and those educated in the Neo-Platonic school require a cautious handling. St. Augustine wrote a whole book of "*Retractations*," and many a Father could have done the same. Thus a few Scripture passages, and a few (or say even a dozen of) passages from the Fathers in support of a doctrine is by no means a sufficient proof of its true Catholic character, unless it is shown that the Bible passages are understood as the Church understands them, and unless the passages from the Fathers are shown to represent the traditional teaching of the Church, and not the personal opinion of man. The Romans but too often forget that there is not only a *Biblical* Protestantism, but also a *Patristic* Protestantism, abusing the Fathers by private judgment, or considering their words as all but inspired truth, whereas the Fathers may only be taken as historical evidences.

Unfortunately it is impossible to the vast majority of Christians to control the testimony taken from the Fathers; and even the few who understand Greek, Latin, Syriac, and Armenian (the four chief languages in which the Fathers have written their works) have neither time nor a mind to read through the voluminous works of the Fathers. Therefore it has become the fashion to consult some patristic supply-stores, collected by busy linguistic ants with little circumspection but with a strong denominational bias. These are the sources of the apparent stupendous learning of the bulk of theologians, who conscientiously propagate the mistakes and misprints of their text-books without taking the trouble of verifying the passages or of finding out their spuriousness or their interpolations. Again, the quotation of a Father is scarcely correctly understood if the Father himself, his place in history, his friends and foes, his studies and associations, his struggles and defeats or victories, his temptations and occasional falls, his religious life, his passions and virtues, and particularly the origin and drift of the work from which the quotation is taken, are unknown to us. On this acquaintance with the Father, as man and Christian, depend virtually the meaning and value of the passage quoted. Thus—to give only one instance of the utter worthlessness of a proof from one of the greatest Fathers and Doctors of the Church—we refer to the well-known passage of St. Jerome (ad Tit. i. 7), in which he tries to show that bishops and priests were identical, and that the distinction proceeded from pride and overbearing. Now we know from history the passionate character of St. Jerome, and how he was revolted at the attempt of a deacon to raise his authority above that of a priest. This induced St. Jerome unduly to exalt the priesthood. Thus the whole argument of St. Jerome being only a product of human passion, is worthless. And what shall we say of St. Jerome's and St. Augustine's mutual imputations of heresy? It shows us that the Fathers must be *studied*, and not simply *quoted*. The Protestants can find, and have found, many passages in the Fathers to support their own errors. From these considerations follows the truth most consolatory to our mind, that all the *pious* Roman Catholics (for there are millions of *nominal* Roman Catholics who are unbelievers or utterly indifferent to religion), who, having neither time nor means or capacity to study the Fathers and to control the proofs adduced by their priests and teachers, continue in an *invincible ignorance*, which they would shake off if they knew better and had no implicit belief in their teachers, virtually belong to us. Therefore we claim them as being *bonâ fide* Orthodox.

To resume the thread of our inquiry. Was Peter simply the President of the co-equal Apostles or their supreme ruler? Peter was avowedly the Primate of the Apostles in order to represent the unity of the Church, as St. Cyprian puts it. Now, was for this purpose a presidency required or a supremacy? What did Peter, in matter of fact, show himself to be? Is it the sign of a ruler to submit to the reprimand of a subject, as Peter did to the reprimand of Paul? Is it a sign of a ruler to be *sent* by his subjects, as Peter was by the other Apostles? Is it the sign of a ruler not to show any authority in the provinces held by his subjects? These are all facts in the life of Peter. And as he acted, so he preached: "Tend the flock of God which is among you, exercising the episcopate (ἐπισκοποῦντες), not of constraint, but willingly, . . . neither as *lording it* over the charge allotted to you, but making yourselves ensamples to the flock." Even the position of Peter's Epistles, nearly at the end of the New Testament Canon, seems not to point to Peter's supremacy.

The Fathers entirely agree with this conclusion. The Apostolic Fathers do not contain the slightest hint at Peter's prerogative, and do not even quote any of the three passages on which this prerogative is based, except St. Luke xxii. 32, quoted in the *interpolated* text of St. Ignatius (ad Smyrn. cap. 7), but explained as referring to all the Apostles, and not to Peter alone. The shorter and authentic text has not the quotation. Now as the Apostolic Fathers show 412 quotations from the New Testament, it must appear strange to us that those remarkable three passages are not among them if the Papal claims had been known to the Primitive Church. At present the Divine right of Papacy is the central dogma of the Roman Church, but of all the Apostolic Fathers only St. Clement mentions even the bare name of Peter, and St. Ignatius (ad Smyrn. 3) mentions "*those who were with Peter*" (τοὺς περὶ Πέτρον), from which words Mr. Allnatt (Cathedra Petri, 2d ed. p. 48) concludes Peter's primacy (!!!) This looks decidedly strange considering the place which Peter occupies at present in the Roman Church.

The numerous passages in which Peter is called *Princeps Apostolorum* mean simply that he was *the first* (princeps) of the Apostles, and not that he was a *Prince* in the meaning of *Ruler*. And likewise πρωτοστάτης and κορυφαῖος signify "one who presides (or stands at the head of) a company." Mr. Allnatt gives further on a wrong translation of πρόκριτος and προκεκριμένος. It is not "*set above*," but "*selected to be the first*." It is altogether unfair to narrow or strain the meaning of words for the benefit of one's pet theory. Thus *caput* and κεφαλή mean "the extreme end of a thing," and not necessarily "the ruling head." The Armenian *kluch* (used by St. James of Nisibis) means not only "the head," but also "*la première place*" (see Aucher's Dictionary). The Hebrew *rosh* and the Chaldaic *resh* mean "the top of a thing." And how little this last expression is fit to denote Papal supremacy we saw from a Syriac MS. of the sixth century, now in the British Museum, in which a treatise of St. Cyril was headed: "*DKurilos resh defiskufe dAleksandria*" (Cyrilli *capitis episcoporum* Alexandriæ), *i.e.*, "Of Cyril Archbishop of Alexandria."

Now let us proceed to give *direct* proof that Peter was not the master of the Apostles but simply their President, *primus inter pares*. Most curiously our chief witness, St. Cyprian, is also claimed by the Romans as theirs. Let the reader then judge which party can justly claim him. Here are the words (De Cath. Eccl. Unitate, caps. 3 and 4): "Upon one He builds His Church; and though He gives to all the Apostles an *equal power*, and says, 'As My Father hath sent Me, even so send I you,' &c.; yet, *in order to manifest unity*, He has by His own authority so placed the source of the same unity as to begin from one. CERTAINLY THE OTHER APOSTLES ALSO WERE WHAT PETER WAS, ENDUED WITH AN EQUAL FELLOWSHIP BOTH OF HONOUR AND POWER; but a commencement is made from unity that the Church may be set before us as one. . . . This unity firmly should we hold and maintain, especially we Bishops presiding in the Church, in order that we may approve the Episcopate itself to be one and undivided." And the Pope—ought he not to have held and maintained this unity, and more firmly still than any other Bishop, since he was the representative of the Church's unity? But he broke the bond and divided the Episcopate. As long as the Pope of Rome and the Episcopate 'dwelt together in unity,' the Pope fulfilled his mission; but when he began to scatter the sheep, he incurred the sentence which St. Peter passed on Judas Iscariot: 'He was numbered with us, and had obtained part of this ministry, . . . (but) let his habitation be desolate, and let no man dwell therein: and his bishopric let another take'! Well may the Pope ponder the following words of Cyprian: "Let no one deceive the brotherhood by falsehood, no one corrupt the truth of our faith by a faithless treachery. *The Episcopate is one, of which a part is held by each without division of the whole.*" And as St. Cyprian taught, so he acted opposite Pope Stephen. Cyprian died *excommunicated by the Pope*, but universally recognised as a saint both by the East and the West, and even by the "infallible Vatican."

St. Gregory of Nyssa, referring to the festival of the Apostles Peter, James, and John, which is celebrated on the same day in the Church of Cappadocia, says that this union is observed "on account of the equality of their dignity" (*διὰ τὸ ὁμότιμον τῆς ἀξίας*").

St. Cyril of Alexandria (Ep. 17) calls Peter and John "of equal dignity" (*ἰσότιμοι ἀλλήλοις*).

The Areopagite (de Eccles. Hier. v. 2, 5) says: "The chief

of the disciples assembled with the other ten hierarchs, who were *of the same rank with him* (*μετὰ τῆς ὁμοταγοῦς αὐτῷ καὶ ἱεραρχικῆς δεκάδος*), to elect the Apostle Matthias."

St. Chrysostom (ad Gal. i. 11): "Paul went to Jerusalem to see Peter. Was there anything more humble than this soul? He did not stand in need of Peter, for he was *his equal* (*ἰσότιμος*)."

And (ad Gal. ii. 3): "He shows himself to be *equal* to the other Apostles; but he compares himself not with the rest, but with the first of them, pointing out that *each had the same dignity.*"

St. John Damascene: "The Apostles form the Holy Ghost's lyre of twelve strings; but neither Peter alone is this lyre, nor Andrew, but *all the twelve together*. IF ANY ONE DECLARES PETER TO BE THIS LYRE, HE IS A LIAR."

The Venerable Bede (Hom. ii. 15): "What was said to Peter, 'Feed my sheep,' was said to all; for *the other Apostles were the same as Peter, but to Peter the Primacy was given, in order that the unity of the Church might be expressed.*"

Isidore of Seville (Hispalensis) says (de Eccl. Off. ii. 5): "The other Apostles shared with Peter *in an equal measure his honour and power*. . . . When they died, they were succeeded by the Bishops who in the whole world were placed on the sees of the Apostles."

This last passage leads us to another class of witnesses, who state that the foundation of the Church was laid in the *Apostolic Sees*, and not only in Peter's See. To this class belongs St. Augustine (cf. Mansi ix. 716) and Pope Pelagius I., who says (Mansi ix. 732): "Whenever a doubt arises . . . let them consult the Apostolic Sees for information. . . . Whoever, therefore, is *separated from the Apostolic Sees is without doubt a schismatic.*" And (716) he teaches "that whoever exempts himself from the authority and communion of the Bishops (*præsulum*) of the same [*i.e.*, the Apostolic] Sees is a schismatic; and that there is no other Church but the one which is grounded in the episcopal roots of the Apostolic Sees (*quæ in pontificibus apostolicarum sedium est solidata radicibus*)." By these passages the present Roman Papacy stands condemned, being separated from all the other Apostolic Sees.

Hitherto we chiefly occupied ourselves with Peter's claims. Now we must go a step farther. The Romans transfer Peter's claims to his pretended successor, the Bishop of Rome. We are sure that Peter's claims never would have been exaggerated had it not been for the benefit of the Pope. But why should Rome have the preference before Antioch, whose first Bishop Peter undoubtedly was, whereas Paul would have an equal right to be considered Bishop of Rome? Here the Roman fallacy begins. Rome became the first Bishopric of Christendom, because it was *the most important city, and, as it were, the centre of the world, hallowed by the martyrdom of the two chief Apostles.* Therefore THE CHURCH (and not Christ or the Apostles) assigned the first place to Rome. This was an *ecclesiastical* arrangement, and not an Apostolic Tradition; consequently it is *no dogma*, for the Church cannot make dogmas. That the Fathers express the highest veneration for such an exalted personage as the Bishop of Rome, and connect him somehow with Peter, who, as it were, hallowed the Roman ground by his martyrdom, is but natural. Moreover, many holy Popes fully deserve our praises as exemplary pastors of the Church. If Peter was only *primus inter pares*, his pretended successors, the Bishops of Rome, cannot be more, whatever some Fathers and many Popes have said. Plain facts refute the exuberant and redundant language of these Fathers. If Œcumenic Councils anathematised Popes as heretics, and Roman Popes had for centuries to repeat these anathemas till they disappeared from the *Liber Diurnus,* it is proof enough that the Œcumenic Council is a higher and safer instance than Papal teaching, and that "Papal Infallibility" is rudely contradicted and exploded by historic facts. And to suppose such an Infallibility, *even without the consent of the Church*, is more than a man of a sound mind can digest. That men like Pius IX., who can say, 'The Tradition is I,' can advance such a heresy, is not wonderful; but that men who are supposed to know more of theology and history can throw their conscience and eternal welfare into the Roman scales, and allow themselves to be blinded and borne down into the fatal abyss, is a mournful sight.

It is *pride* that caused the fall of angels (1 Tim. iii. 6). It is *pride* that caused the fall of man. When the tempter's words, "*Ye shall be as gods*," had poisoned Eve's heart, covetousness and lust freely entered. And this pride was a *lie*, or rather *the* lie, the parent-lie of all subsequent lies, for it was the usurpation of God's supremacy by beings created by God and dependent on God. Therefore our Saviour says that the fallen angel, the Devil, "abode not in the truth, because there is no truth in him. When he speaketh a lie, he speaketh of his own: for he is a liar, and the father of it" (St. John viii. 44). As the Devil's *pride and lie* entered the *Church of Paradise*, but could not prevail against it, since Adam and Eve, as repentant sinners, clung to the promised Saviour, so the devil of *lying pride* has persistently continued harassing and ravaging the Church of God, and will continue doing so till doomsday. It was his *lying pride* that seduced the children of Israel into idolatry, annihilated the ten tribes, and crucified Jesus Christ. It is his *lying pride* that persecuted Christ, even after His death, in His disciples, originated heresies and produced schisms. It is his *lying pride* that invented *Papal Supremacy and Infallibility* as the blasting-engine to destroy Christ's Church. But, as in the Old Testament, he succeeded in carrying away with him ten of the twelve tribes, so in the Christian Church the majority followed him as their leader. With what result we shall presently see.

Great things usually grow from small beginnings. And so it is with Papacy. The Devil was far too clever to introduce all at once full-blown Papacy, for he was certain that Christendom would directly have discovered the cloven foot of its author. He preferred sowing the tares during the night, "while men slept." The weeds grew up with the wheat, at first scarcely to be distinguished from each other. And when both could be distinguished, the weeds were too deep-rooted to be easily eradicated, and the eyes of the people were accustomed to the harmless look of the poisonous plant, and to the religious halo surrounding the same; for the Devil frequently appears as an *angel of light.*

It is a significant fact that the first record of the Pope's doctrinal authority of the *Cathedra Petri* is to be found in an *heretical work of fiction* of the latter half of the second century, the *Clementine Homilies*, written by an Ebionite. In this interesting novel Peter is for the first time connected with the See of Rome to the exclusion of Paul. He addresses himself to the Romans, saying, "I consecrate this Clement as your Bishop, *to whom I confide my chair of teaching*" (ᾧ τὴν ἐμὴν τῶν λόγων πιστεύω καθέδραν). However, the Clementines did not attribute the Primacy to Peter, but to James, the Bishop of Jerusalem. The waning influence of Jerusalem naturally brought about the transfer of the Primacy to Rome. A condensation, or rather recasting of the Clementines, called "Recognitions," written in the beginning of the third century, and equally issuing from *heretic* quarters, was widely circulated and eagerly read. Thus two *heretic novels* were the fountain or cradle of Papal Supremacy, wrapt in the swaddling-cloth of the Ebionite, Elkesaite, and Artemonite heresies. The Orthodox contemporaries of these heterodox novels, St. Dionysius of Corinth and St. Irenæus, did not know of a *Cathedra Petri* at Rome, but ascribed the foundation of the Church of Rome to both Peter and Paul.

However, the seed of the serpent, disseminated by the two heretic novels, sprang speedily up. Pope Victor sent, in 196, threatening letters into the provinces where Easter was kept with the Jews on the 14th of Nisan, and "tries" (πειρᾶται) to excommunicate the Easterns, who, however, resisted to a man. His third predecessor, Anicetus, had, thirty years before, treated the same question with St. Polycarp, but, though disagreeing, they parted in peace. So much Papal ambition had already grown in the meanwhile. Victor was defeated along the whole line, for as to his pretended supreme power he had no traditional ground to stand upon. But the Popes Zephyrinus and Stephen had already a precedent in Victor, though also their pretensions were universally rejected. If any one here objects that Victor's and Stephen's views on the particular doctrine or practice they defended prevailed in the end, we answer that Victor withal was an abettor of the heretic Praxeas, and the Pope Zephyrinus and his successor Callistus were Noetians. Thus we have at the outset three heretic Popes on the Cathedra Petri. Hitherto the Papal pretensions were rejected; but with every ambitious Pope the number of precedents grew, and the number of arguments too; for ambition and imperiousness are most ingenious in finding out plausible reasons and evidences in favour of their proceedings, and "frustrate the truth by subtilty" (*veritatem subtilitate frustrantur*), as St. Cyprian says. Or, to quote Dr. Newman's words ("On Development," p. 92): "And thus we see opinions, usages, and systems, *which are of venerable and imposing aspect, but which have no soundness within them, and keep together from a habit of consistence.*" Papacy went on briskly, conquered both the ecclesiastical and the secular world, pleaded the *jus præscriptionis*, and built up a system of Papal rights in spite of powerful Councils contesting the same. But how can a *lie* become a prescriptive right? "Custom without truth is an old error" (Consuetudo sine veritate, *vetustas erroris est*), says St. Cyprian.

People are generally labouring under the delusion that the first centuries of the Church were the palmy days of Christendom; that the description of the zeal in the young Church of Jerusalem, as we read in the Acts of the Apostles, and the glowing picture we admire in the Epistle addressed by a disciple of the Apostles to Diognetus, entitle us to consider the early Christians as a band of saints. This was by no means the case. St. Paul and St. Clement disclose a state of affairs in the Church of Corinth as we see in Christendom in our own time. And of the Seven Churches of Asia, to which St. John addresses his Revelation, there is only one, the Church of Philadelphia, that is not more or less severely rebuked. And the Church of Laodicea is a true type of hundreds of Churches of the nineteenth century. The Church of Rome was well spoken of at the time of St. Paul, and there are several reasons which account for it: (1.) The stock of the Christian community at Rome consisted of Jews, hated and despised by the heathens, and therfore socially excluded and providentially guarded against the enormous immorality of the surrounding heathendom. (2.) The frequent persecutions, fiercer in the capital than anywhere else, kept the right spirit up. However, there is no doubt that in the course of time, when the Christians increased, and many foreign elements associated with the old stock, when the Roman Church grew important and influential, and participated, as it were, in the unique position of heathen Rome, the Mistress of the World, Christian Rome assumed a more secular aspect. Power and influence beget pride, ambition, and intrigue. And these, indeed, were already in full swing long before the end of the persecutions in the latter half of the second century. If any one of our readers will consult St. Hippolytus's admirable work "Refutation of all Heresies" (the first seven chapters of the ninth book), he will see how the Church of Rome, under the Popes Zephyrinus and Callistus, was a hotbed of intrigues and heresies, ruled by unworthy and venal Popes. *Romæ omnia venalia*—just as in our days. Now a word about Hippolytus. He is a recognised saint of the undivided Church, a disciple of St. Irenæus, a contemporary of Zephyrinus and Callistus, an eye-witness of what he relates. Of course the Ultramontane Infallibilists were furious when the work mentioned was found in 1850. But other works of St. Hippolytus were known before, and the highest praise was bestowed upon our author, whom St. Jerome ranks among the very first of the Fathers. No doubt about his orthodoxy was entertained. Such is the judgment of the Roman Catholics Möhler, Bishop Fessler, Gruscha, &c. Anastasius Bibliothecarius calls him *sacratissimum et magnum Doctorem veritatisque testem fidelem.* The above-mentioned work appeared in 1851, and fell like a thunderbolt into the midst of the Ultramontanes. Suddenly their tactics changed, and in order to clear their Popes and save their new-fangled dogma, they construed history, not from facts, but from the depth of their inner consciousness, *i.e.*, they manufactured history as they wished it to have been, declared St. Hippolytus to have been a schismatic, but to have been reconciled to the

Church before his death. These are *two inventions* without the slightest historic foundation.* Of course it is very painful to the heart of a tender Infallibilist to see St. Cyprian, St. Hippolytus, St. Meletius of Antioch dying outside the pale of the Papal Church, yet recognised and venerated by this Papal Church as Saints, a clear sign that the communion with the Pope was not a requisite for eternal salvation, but sometimes an impediment—then, namely, when the Popes were heretics or usurped undue power.

Under the subsequent Popes the development of the Papal claims went on, if at all, very slowly; in fact, too slowly for the taste of the later Papists, so that they thought themselves entitled to help and correct history by *forging* some Papal Decretals, which were readily believed and circulated. Thus the basis of Papal Supremacy, which is a *lie*, could only be supported by a string of lies. And this string was certainly made as tight as possible; for from Callistus's successor, Urban I., every Pope was fitted out with forged epistles, so that to the Popes from Urban I. to Melchiades not less than *thirty forged epistles* were ascribed. Of course Callistus's predecessors were likewise decorated with forgeries (twenty-seven pieces). This is the real groundwork of the present Papal Church.

We saw at the time of the Popes Victor, Zephyrinus, and Callistus a marked change in the Roman Church, as described by St. Paul. It had now become a resort of heretics, an arena of all the lowest passions, of bribes and corruption. Yet the time of persecution had not yet passed, and the very persecutions were only a blessing of Heaven to purify the foul air accumulated in the Church during the lull between the storms. But scarcely the persecutions had passed when Ammianus Marcellinus (xxvii. 3) severely blames the Roman Bishops for *giving banquets and dinner-*

---

* It is to Dr. Döllinger, the subtlest advocate of the Papal Church before he left it, that the Roman Church owes this master-stroke. He combines several stray notices of rather doubtful value, which have little or nothing to do with our subject, and forms them into a string of purely conjectural evidences. This is the way Roman Catholic historians are nowadays compelled to adopt in order to overcome the barriers which plain history opposes to their doctrinal innovations. However these tricks may charm and satisfy a professional juggler, they cannot convince a sincere student of historical truth.

parties which were more sumptuous than royal banquets. But he adds that "some Bishops in the provinces" were still left who led a truly Apostolic life. Ammian Marcellinus, though a heathen, is admitted on all hands, even by the most fastidious Roman Catholic, to excel by his stern impartiality and love of truth. Thus it was at his time (the latter half of the fourth century), not in Rome, where you had to look for the pattern of Christianity, but in remote provinces, where the infection of Roman *worldliness* had not yet spread. What Ammian Marcellinus tells us is confirmed by St. Jerome (Epist. ad Nepotian. ep. 6 *seq.*), who bitterly complains of the vanity, pomp, assuming of importance, and particularly of the pompous meals, of the Bishops of his time.

Dr. Newman, "On Development," p. 22 *seq.*, admits that the Ante-Nicene testimonies for Papal Supremacy are *faint*, or, as we must confess, *imaginary.* We have given an exhaustive commentary on the passage in our "Catholic Orthodoxy" (London, Trübner, 1866), pp. 123–172, and beg to refer the reader to it. But if Dr. Newman thinks he may construe his faint outlines into a *cumulative* argument, he is mistaken. Naughts may count, indeed, but only if attached to a real quantity. Standing by themselves they disappear into thin air. Moreover, Papal Supremacy is a doctrine which is unique and quite peculiar among the other doctrines, since it must be either *nothing* or *all*, *i.e.*, either a *figment* or *the foundation* of the Church. Plain common sense tells every reasonable person that a foundation cannot possibly be developed in the course of centuries from faint outlines, *while the building is all the while firmly established, victoriously weathering the fiercest storms.* If Papal Supremacy (necessarily and logically including Infallibility) were a dogma, it would be the *central* dogma, because the existence of the whole Church, with all her dogmas, would depend on it. Consequently Papal Supremacy would have been, of a necessity, *the first dogma* taught and insisted upon on admitting anybody into the Church. Thus the Apostles acted *incorrectly* in summoning a Council and allowing St. James to preside and proclaim the sentence, instead of simply applying to

Peter. Thus the Œcumenic Councils acted *wrongly* in assuming to themselves the Infallibility which strictly belonged only to the Pope, and in anathematising even Popes. And the Popes *submitted* to the synodal verdict, and anathematised for centuries their own "infallible" predecessors!!! Could those Popes possibly have had the slightest inkling of what the Papal Church believes at present? And if they had not, the foundation of their Church was *defective*, and the building on a *defective* foundation could not be Christ's *indestructible* Church.

The first deed of Papal Supremacy was enacted by Pope Victor in 196, and *although repudiated by the Church as a usurpation, and practically a failure* (since Victor was compelled to yield), it created a *precedent*, which his successors were not slow in catching hold of, as we see in Stephen's pontificate. Stephen went a step farther, and really excommunicated the African Church, which, however, did not heed it; but Dionysius of Alexandria, one of the most illustrious Fathers of the time, blamed him for it. It is in this way that, step by step, a Papal tradition grew up, based on precedents, and bequeathing to every successor the Papal heirloom of all the centuries past. A strong *esprit de corps* naturally animated Popedom, which concentrated in itself all the elements of *a Church within the Church*, which idea, in later times, the Jesuits fully realised.

Our adversaries will here object: "If Papacy had been such an institution, how could men like Leo the Great and Gregory the Great, recognised as Saints by the Church, have upheld such an institution?" No doubt, both these Popes were staunch upholders of the Papal Primacy, and it is no use denying that they saw in the Primacy something more than a simple Presidency. This was their PERSONAL OPINION, and as long as they did not force it on the Church as a *dogma*, excommunicating those who held another view, they were fully at liberty to indulge in their particular thoughts. We are perfectly sure that SS. Leo and Gregory, if they saw the present development of Papacy, would detest and reject it as we do. We should find them at Constantinople and not at Rome. They would be in communion with

Joakim III., and not with Leo XIII. However, the growth of Papacy in the ante-schismatic times is partly due to the Easterns themselves, since in their *complimentary flatteries* and abject deference to the Popes they used frequently terms bordering on cringing servility, which Rome took in full earnest in order to make capital of it. So Justinian calls Pope John II. "the head of all the holy Churches" (*caput omnium sanctarum ecclesiarum*), but in Cod. Just. i. 2, 25, we read, "The Constantinopolitan Church is the head of all the other Churches" (*ἡ ἐν Κωνσταντινουπόλει ἐκκλησία πασῶν τῶν ἄλλων ἐστὶ κεφαλή*). We could make a string of such contradictory expressions. But suffice it to say that words must be measured by deeds, and that *actions* are the most reliable interpreters of *words*. Now the Easterns, though occasionally hoaxing and coaxing the Popes with a superabundance of sweet and sonorous titles, such as vain and ambitious people like to hear, were all along most firm and consistent in their actions. In this respect Photius was not more determined than St. John Chrysostom was, and St. Basil was even so keen-sighted as to discover the fatal root of the evil—viz., "*Western superciliousness*" (*ὀφρὺς δυτική*). It is not by a show of laudatory passages from the Fathers, but by the plain course of history that the Papal claims are to be decided.

The first indisputable allusion to the authority of the Bishop of Rome is to be found in the 6th Canon of the first Council of Nicæa, in which the privileges of the Head-Metropolitans (afterwards called Patriarchs) of Alexandria and Antioch were confirmed, since *old custom* (*τὰ ἀρχαῖα ἔθη*) had assigned such rights to them, and "since this *custom* also obtains (*σύνηθές ἐστιν*) with regard to the Bishop of Rome." Thus "Custom" and not "Dogma" regulated the position of the Bishop of Rome. The Romans here reply that we must distinguish the threefold character of the Pope viz., that of a Bishop of Rome, that of a Patriarch of the West, and that of the universal Pope. They say: The Patriarchal rights of the Pope were indeed an institution grown up by custom, without being in the least *derogatory* to the Divine prerogative of Papacy. This is a rather transparent fallacy, not to say a downright Jesuitical mystification. If the Popes, during the whole period of undivided Christendom, did not dare to appoint and consecrate a Bishop for Constantinople, Antioch, Babylon, Nicomedia, or any other place in the East (*as they do now, flagrantly violating the Holy Canons*), who has given them this increase of power, which their holy predecessors, by anticipation, unsparingly condemned? Thus St. Leo the Great (Ep. 62 ad Maximum Antiochenum Episcopum) says: "The tranquillity of universal peace cannot be otherwise preserved, unless the reverence due to the Canons is kept inviolate." (*Universæ pacis tranquillitas non aliter poterit custodiri, nisi sua canonibus reverentia intemerata servetur.*) According to the present notion of Papacy, the Pope can override and overrule the Holy Canons. Consequently *the Papacy of St. Leo was a totally different thing from what is now styled Papacy*. If the present Papist will be consistent, he must admit that what he considers the inherent rights of Papacy never must have been disowned by the predecessors of the present Pope. Again, if the Œcumenic Councils and the Holy Canons derived their authority from the assent of the Pope, how could Popes submit to them, even if their verdict was against them? The present state of Papal development confesses that, strictly speaking, Œcumenic Councils are *superfluous*, since the infallible voice emanates solely from the Pope. Consequently the Church would, from the times of the Apostles, have performed a farce playing at Council without possessing the gift of infallibility, claimed and unanimously taught by the Church of undivided Christendom. "But (the Infallibilists will reply) the Œcumenic Councils, *as soon as confirmed by the Pope*, were really infallible." No, they were not; for it was only the word of the Pope borrowing the decisions of the Council and making them his own, as he might have borrowed the words of any book, or of any private councillor, even of a heretic. But would you call that book, or that councillor, or that heretic *infallible* because the Pope proclaimed what he had borrowed from them to be infallible truth?

It must be very humiliating to the Infallibilists that the

first Œcumenic Council was neither convoked, nor presided over, nor confirmed by the Pope or his delegates. In fact, the Roman delegates played very subordinate parts; wherefore the Papal historians tried to introduce Hosius of Cordova as a sort of Papal representative, though history only knows him as a favourite courtier of the Emperor. The Pope, indeed, accepted the Council, but he *neither confirmed nor was asked to confirm the Council.* Now there is this difference—a subject accepts, a superior confirms. That the Romans were by no means content with the scanty consideration of their Pope in the 6th Canon we see from the many interpolations in the different Latin translations beginning the Canon by the words, "The Roman Church possessed always the Primacy" (*Ecclesia Romana semper habuit primatum*), or similar expressions.

Peter Ballerini (a classical author in all that concerns the pretended Papal prerogative) contends in his book, "*De potestate Ecclesiastica Summorum Pontificum et Conciliorum Generalium*" (Romæ, 1850), p. 71, that the œcumenicity of a Council depends on whether it is duly convoked by the Pope. Now the first Council of Nicæa can show no proof that it was convoked by the Pope. The Ultramontanes object that no counter-proof could be produced, since the letter of convocation was lost. Fortunately this letter was since discovered by B. Harris Cowper (*Analecta Nicæna*, London, 1857) in an old Syriac translation dating from the latter half of the fifth century. The manuscript is to be found in the British Museum (Add. MSS. No. 14,523, fol. 146; another MS. of the letter we find in Add. MSS. No. 14,526). In this letter the Emperor Constantine does not mention the Pope, but only "the Bishops of Italy and of the rest of the countries of Europe." That Pope Sylvester and Emperor Constantine "*collected*" (συνέλεγον) the Bishops of the Council (as the sixth Œcumenic Council affirms) may be true enough, but has nothing to do with the Convocation of the Council. How independently Constantine acted in this respect even in the very city of Rome, we see from his summoning the Roman Council under Pope Melchiades in 313 (Euseb. Hist. Eccles. x. 5, and Vita Constantini I., 44).

But as our limited space does not allow us to enter farther into this question, we refer the reader to our article, "The Impending so-called Œcumenical Council of the Roman Church" (*Orthodox Catholic Review*, vol. ii. 1869, pp. 103–116). In this article we have minutely examined, at the hand of history, the Papal claim of convoking Œcumenical Councils.

We saw how the history of the first Œcumenic Council by no means corroborates, but rather contradicts, the claims of the Papacy of our days. The second Œcumenic Council, the first of Constantinople, is still more opposed to these Papal claims, *i.e.*, showed plainly that such claims were totally unknown in the East. The Romans admit that this Council was not convoked by the Pope; that it was successively presided over by three Bishops who were opposed to Rome, St. Meletius of Antioch, St. Gregory of Nazianzus, and Nectarius; that the Synod which was held in Constantinople the following year (382) recognised it as an Œcumenic Council. The West did not recognise it for some time, because it consisted exclusively of Easterns. We have shown in our article just referred to (p. 107 *seq.*) that this was the fault of the Westerns, who were duly invited, but did not come. Theodoret (Hist. Eccl. v. 8) tells us that the Easterns resented this *neglect* by *refusing* to be present at a General Council to be held at Rome, and presided over by the Pope himself. This latter Council, *under the entire management of the Pope*, was never recognised as an Œcumenic Council, but our Council, *opposed by the Pope*, was soon recognised by the whole Catholic world. This fact speaks volumes. The Romans used, indeed, their familiar weapon "*forgery*" to hide their defeat by declaring Paschasinus, Lucentius, and Bonifacius to have attended the Council as Papal Legates (Mansi, Collect. Concil. tom. vi. p. 1176). Unfortunately these men attended *seventy* years later the Council of Chalcedon!! Our Council was indirectly recognised as œcumenic already in 38? by Pope Damasus, for in approving the Constantinopolitan Council of 382 (which expressly and emphatically declares that of 381 to have been an Œcumenic Council), he approves also its statement. The Popes Vigilius and Pelagius II. count it among the Œcumenical Councils, and St. Gregory the Great venerated the Councils of Nicæa, Constantinople, Ephesus, and Chalcedon "as the four books of the holy Gospel." Yet the same St. Gregory says that the disciplinary Canons of the Council are not to be found in the Roman Church. Oh, yes! documents sometimes disappear from the Papal archives, as Father Aug. Theiner in his history of the Pontificate of Clement XIV. has abundantly proved. Perhaps the last session of the Council of Chalcedon offers a clue to it. At all events, the communication of Eusebius of Doryleum throws a strange light on Pope Leo I. Besides, there is plenty of reason for the disappearance of these Canons, since the second and the third must have been decidedly unpalatable to Roman tastes, for the second did scarcely leave any room for appeals to Rome, and the third in assigning to the Bishop of Constantinople "the first place (τὰ πρεσβεῖα) of honour after the Bishop of Rome, *because* that (city) is New Rome," implied the human origin and merely customary precedence of the Pope, *because* he was Bishop of Old Rome. The Papal tradition, so lustily developing under the shadow of "Peter's chair," fed by precedents, supported by forgeries, educated by a judicious selection of patristic passages, drilled by ecclesiastical skirmishes, had grown up to the stature of a vigorous youth, when all at once the East stepped forward and contested its very existence, its *raison d'être*, stripped off its Divine mask, and levelled it down to the state of a *figment!*

The finishing stroke to Rome's suprematial pretensions was given by the 28th Canon of the Œcumenical Council of Chalcedon in 451. It runs as follows:—"In every respect following the decrees of the holy Fathers, and knowing the recently recited Canon of the 150 God-beloved Bishops [of the second Œcumenic Council], we also resolve and decree the same concerning the pre-eminence of the most Holy Church of Constantinople, New Rome, since the Fathers justly attributed to the throne of elder Rome the pre-eminence, because that city is an Imperial capital, and moved by the same motive the 150 God-beloved Bishops have awarded the same pre-eminence to the holiest throne of New Rome, with full reason of judging that the city honoured by the Imperial government and Senate, and enjoying equal pre-eminence as elder Imperial Rome, is also in ecclesiastical affairs exalted, being the second after her. . . ." This Canon is clear with a vengeance, and the Papists for once understood it properly, because there was no possibility of misunderstanding, obscuring, or distorting it. Two hundred Bishops were present and signed the Canon. Now if these two hundred had known anything of a *Divine right* of Papacy, could they have dared to place Constantinople on the same level with Rome? Or would they not have hinted at the dogmatic line of demarcation? Or were they ignorant men and bad theologians? The Acts of the Council do not prove it, but just the reverse. Or were they two hundred wicked men, driven perhaps by jealousy to defraud Rome of its rights? If this had been the case, how shall we explain that the whole Eastern Church, with all her saints and learned doctors, remained faithful to this Canon from 451 to 1881, in spite of Rome's protesting against it for centuries? Here the advocates of Papal Supremacy are absolutely at a dead-lock. Give us ten score of patristic passages supporting Rome's claims, beautiful *words!* We prefer one *action* of 1400 years' duration. We prefer *solid reality* to a *sham fabric.* Let here the Roman pause and bethink himself!

Pope Leo I. stoutly resisted the 28th Canon of Chalcedon, and used such strong language as Pius IX. might have used. Yet Leo was not a Papist in the modern sense of the word, and this for two reasons: First, he thought our 28th Canon contradicted the 6th Canon of Nicæa, and as he considered it his chief office to be *Guardian of the Holy Canons*, he resisted this ostensible encroachment of a later Council on the right of a former. Thus Leo was a *bonâ fide* defender of what he considered to be an imprescriptible right. Yet Leo was mistaken, since one Œcumenical Council can alter (and has repeatedly altered) the disciplinary arrangements of another according to the requirements of the time. Now, as the Roman Church recognises the same principle, our opponent will contend, with some show of probability, that Leo must have considered the Papal question not as a matter of changeable discipline, but of unchangeable dogma. This naturally leads us to the second point. Had Leo believed that the 28th Canon violated a dogma, it would have been his *duty* to *anathematise* the two hundred Bishops who issued it, and all their contemporary and subsequent adherents. But neither Leo or any of his successors did so, however provoked they felt sometimes. Is this not a clear proof that *the Divine right of Papal Supremacy* was at that time not believed to be a *dogma?* Now, this is sufficient for us Orthodox, who believe that *what was once not a dogma can never become one.* The Apostolic deposit of faith once delivered to the Saints cannot increase or decrease, cannot be developed or be reduced, but is the old well-known heirloom of our fathers, the jewel (*κειμήλιον*) watched and looked at every day, and shown to our children in every catechetical instruction. We need not paste a new leaf in the older editions of our Catechism in order to insert a new dogma. Our Catechisms never are antiquated, because their contents date from the times of the Apostles. We have neither a mediæval scholastic school under the leadership of Thomas Aquinas, nor Roman Congregations to prepare and fashion dogmas for us. We are poor in dogmas as compared with Rome. We are despised in our old-fashioned clothes (our dogmas and canons) as compared with the modern cut of the Roman garb. Never mind; our material is genuine and substantial. Only children and fools like tinsel and tawdry ornaments, such as the Roman factory of dogmas, constitutions, bulls, breves, &c., produces, particularly in the matter of indulgences, miracles, and scapularies.

St. Leo did not anathematise his Eastern dissentients, therefore he belongs to us, and not to the present Papists of the West. Leo's successors continued protesting against the 28th Canon of Chalcedon, which was reconfirmed by the 36th Canon of the Synod in Trullo. If Hefele thinks that Pope Felix III. even excommunicated Acacius, Patriarch of Constantinople, on account of the 28th Canon of Chalcedon, he is decidedly wrong, for the excommunication was simply the consequence of Acacius's advocating the Henoticon, which slighted the Council of Chalcedon. At last Eastern constancy silenced the Popes; the controversy was no longer touched, and seemed to have altogether disappeared, when suddenly Rome, "*renewing the ancient privileges of the Patriarchal Sees*," adopted in substance the 28th canon of Chalcedon. This happened in 1215, in the fourth Lateran Council (5th Canon) under Pope Innocent III. Thus what St. Leo had so loudly denounced as derogatory to the 6th Canon of Nicæa was spontaneously adopted by the really Ultramontane Popes about 800 years later. How are we to account for it? Has at last the Pope been converted to the Eastern views or repented of his obstinacy? Nothing of the sort. Rome does nothing but for reasons of self-interest. A Latin empire had been founded in Constantinople and a Latin Patriarch installed, an obedient servant of the Pope. Thus in "renewing" the ancient Patriarchal privileges, Rome only secured an extent of its own power and influence. Rome did not mind eating its own words and forgetting its own protests, provided it could thereby make a nice profit. The breach between the East and the West had been consummated since more than a century, and "ancient privileges of the Patriarchal Sees," *never recognised before*, could safely be admitted.

But we must return to that fatal epoch when the fuel for a universal conflagration in the Church had so accumulated that the slightest spark was sure to set the whole house on fire. Rome had innovated in doctrine and discipline to such a degree that only a rupture could save the sound body of the Eastern Church from Western infection. However, we may confidently say that the questions about the Filioque, Indulgences, Purgatory, &c., could and would have been settled had not the question of *self-interest*, *of power*, *of dominion*, *of pride*—in short, had not the question of *Papal Supremacy* prevented any readjustment. Up to the year 863 the difference between Photius and Pope Nicholas I. might have been composed. But between 863 and 865 an event took place which altered the whole aspect of affairs, namely, the

Pseudo-Isidorian Decretals fell at this time into the hands of Nicholas, were readily accepted, and became henceforth the rule of Papal action.

The Pseudo-Isidorian Decretals were *the most extensive, most important, and most impudent fraud ever perpetrated in history.* And on this basis the theory of *the Divine right of Papal Supremacy* rests; out of this *lie* the *dogma* of Papal Supremacy grew up, and was proclaimed as such in 1215 (fourth Lateran Council, which the Romans consider as an Œcumenical Council). Thus the first seed of Papal Supremacy, sown by a *heretic* novel (the Clementines), matured by successive acts of pride, ambition, and dominion, had been brought to its final development into a dogma by the most abominable *forgery* on record.

Let us quote here some remarks of a French Jesuit paper (cf. *Orthodox Catholic Review*, vol. ii. pp. 195–199): "This new discipline . . . adopted by Nicholas in 865, by the eighth [so-called] Œcumenical Council in 870, confirmed by the Council of Trent in 1564, has been for nine centuries the common right of the Catholic Church; *but it is impossible to justify, or even to excuse, the means employed by Pseudo-Isidore to attain his end. Untruth remains an evil, even when he who employs it means well. And the falsehood was premeditated! . . . It must be acknowledged that a more audacious, important, solemn, and persevering untruth has never been put forth, and, let us add, one for centuries so triumphant. Yes, the impostor gained his end; he produced a change of discipline as he desired, but he did not arrest the general decline. God does not bless imposture. . . .* Who can say what canonical literature might now be if the Burchard of Worms, the Anselm of Lucias, and the Yves of Chartres, if Gratian himself, instead of drawing their inspiration from the false Decretals, had been guided in their labours by the 'Hispana,' with its logical, simple, and luminous table of contents!" There is scarcely any Roman Catholic who does not fully recognise the fraudulent character of these Decretals, yet *the Roman Church has up to the present moment not yet publicly and officially disavowed them!!!* But how could an "*infallible*" Church confess its wrong, since its "*infallible*"

Popes ruled the same by *forgeries* for nine centuries? It is only a bad cause which requires the helping hand of the forger. Now the Roman Church became a regular *manufactory of forgeries.* The works of the Fathers were tampered with on a grand scale—spurious works attributed to them—interpolations introduced—unpleasant passages discarded. It is no use denying or minimising this charge. Patent facts speak too loudly. Read the Acts of the Council of Florence, edited by a Benedictine monk (Nickes ?), Rome, 1864 (Greek), 1865 (Latin), and you will see the confusion of the Roman members of the Council when one patristic evidence after another was proved by the Greeks to be a forgery. And the Benedictine editor of St. Basil's works justly remarks: "How many evils have, both formerly and in the present day, sprung up from hence [*i.e.*, from tampering with the Fathers], every one who is not altogether unexperienced in ecclesiastical matters, fully knows,—*doctrines are obscured, morals are polluted, history falters, tradition is disturbed;* and, to express my meaning in a word, if once the genuine writings of the Holy Fathers are confounded with the adulterous ones, all things must necessarily be confounded together." Zörnikaw, in his classical work on the Procession of the Holy Ghost (2d and 3d treatises) points out twenty-five falsifications in the Greek Fathers, and forty-three in the Latin; but as the Latin forgeries were too numerous, he treats them under the heading, "*Corruptelæ variæ de ingenti numero unico argumento demonstrantur*" (pp. 98–309). It is a significant fact that the overwhelming majority of forgeries concerns Papal Supremacy, and that St. Cyprian is chosen as the chief focus of forgeries. More than twenty spurious works were attributed to him. And the text of his genuine works, though now critically purified and settled, continues to be quoted by eminent Roman theologians in its interpolated form, *e.g.*, by J. Cardoni in his "Elucubratio de Dogmatica Rom. Pont. Infallibilitate eiusque Definibilitate, Romæ, 1870," p. 36. The Roman Catholic William Palmer ("Dissertations on the Orthodox Communion," p. 147), says: "The general practice of Roman Catholic writers has been to defend all the existing doctrines of their Church, and (on the most important points) her discipline also, and ritual, on the ground of tradition, either written or oral, preserved uninterruptedly from the beginning. Enslaved to this theory, *they have too often interpolated and corrupted the text of ancient authors, denied or explained away their plain meaning, and given a false colouring to ecclesiastical history.*" This peep into the working machinery of the Roman Church will, no doubt, cure some single-minded and earnest Roman Catholics, who hitherto believed that their Church was *the abode of the Spirit of Truth,* instead of *the workshop of the Father of Lies*—instead of "the *abomination of desolation standing in the holy place.*"—Come out of Babylon! Come, and do not tarry!

It was on the 16th of July 1054, when the Papal Legates deposited on the altar of Hagia Sophia at Constantinople the Bull of Excommunication, that Rome cut itself off from *the One true Church of Christ.* This suicidal act of self-inflicted doom was, however, too serious to be all at once realised by the West. Pope Alexander II. (1072) considered the union of both the Churches as still existing. Even Pope Gregory VII. only complains that the love between both Churches had grown cold (*quod utrimque eorum caritas friguit,* Epist. lib. i. 18). The last instance of implicit recognition of the Orthodox Church is to be found in a letter of Peter, Abbot of Clugny, to the Patriarch, John IX. Chalcedonius, in 1119. So strong was the bond of brotherly love, so strong the habit of living and worshipping together for a thousand years, so great the wickedness of the tearing in pieces of "the seamless tunic of the Lord," that it took more than half a century for the West to realise the fatal event. And even now, after an estrangement of 800 years, the Greek remembers that they once were brothers, but that the unnatural Roman brother forfeited his rights and privileges, like the prodigal son of the Gospel. How long will the latter still live on the husks of human conceits?

It is wonderful how, from the time when Pope Nicholas I. tried to bring about the divorce between the two Churches, the downward course of Rome proceeded with such a rapidity that one could not but recognise God's finger on the wall, "*Mene, mene, tekel, upharsin!*"

It was Nicholas who introduced the Pseudo-Isidorian Decretals, this Trojan horse of the Roman Church. And his successor, Hadrian II., succeeded in having the Pseudo-Isidorian principles (these legalised lies) recognised by the (so-called) Œcumenical Council of Constantinople (869), which was packed for the occasion. There can scarcely be found a more miserable sham than this Council, in which three disguised Saracen merchants were slily introduced to act as the representatives of the Patriarchs of Alexandria, Antioch, and Jerusalem, as we learn from the evidence of the Patriarchs themselves in the Synod of 879. Eleven years later Formosus, Bishop of Porto, ascended the Papal throne. The Popes had long since forgotten St. Paul's injunction (2 Tim. ii. 4) "not to entangle themselves in the affairs of this life." Their greediness of power was, naturally enough, not confined to ecclesiastical concerns; they strove also to become powerful political agents. Formosus was succeeded by Stephen VI. (for Boniface the Sixth's pontificate of fifteen days can scarcely be counted), who, being a fanatic partisan of the opposite political faction, had Formosus untombed, dressed in pontifical robes, arraigned, condemned, deposed, mutilated, and finally flung into the Tiber! This behaviour seems not exactly to be in accordance with the character of a "Vicar of Christ." However, the Papists have to settle this question. We prefer examining the Council convened by Stephen for the before-mentioned purpose. In this Council. Stephen declared all ordinations made by Formosus to be *invalid*, and acted accordingly. This was not a private, but an *official act*, attended by *official consequences*, and, what is more serious, it was an official act based on a *dogmatic error;* in fact, it was an anticipation of the *heresy of John Huss.* And the Church continued for two years in this heresy! Yet the Romans are bound to believe that Stephen was an "infallible" Pope. Pope John IX. annulled, in 898, the decrees of Stephen, declared the ordinations made by Formosus to be valid, and reinstated the expelled clergy. The only difficulty is to come here to a decision which of the two "Infallibles" is the genuine article, and even then the base article must be believed by the Romans to be *infallible.* Who is able to get out of this maze of contradictions?

From 904–963, the πορνοκρατία, or "reign of prostitutes," disgraced the Papal throne. From Sergius III. to John XII. eleven monsters of lewdness and profligacy ruled the Church of God, persons utterly indifferent to religion and poisoning Christendom by their bad example. Sergius III. had no scruple in sanctioning the sacrilegious marriage of the Byzantine Emperor Leo VI., but the Patriarch Nicholas Mysticus had vindicated the purity of the Church by excommunicating the Emperor, who, with the help of Pope Sergius, deposed the undaunted and faithful Patriarch. If the Roman Church was the true Church, and the Pope the factotum of this Church, where was the Holy Ghost governing the Church during these sixty years?

Now let us cast a glance on the Patriarchs of Constantinople during the period of the Roman πορνοκρατία. *All of them, six in number, were men of an exemplary sanctity*, with the solitary exception of Theophylact, who was *a creature of Pope John XII., and was installed by the Papal Legates.* He was the worst Patriarch that ever sat on the Constantinopolitan throne. Do these contrasts not convey any lesson to us? With which of the two parties was God?

It is a consequence of original sin that the natural man hankers after greatness, power, and dominion. So it was also the case with the Apostles. On two occasions the Apostles discussed the question, "which of them should be greatest." On the first occasion (St. Luke ix. 46), it was only a διαλογισμὸς, "a reasoning among them." On the second occasion (St. Luke xxii. 24), it had grown already into a φιλονεικία, "a strife and contention." In both cases Jesus rebuked them. That Peter must have taken a prominent part in the discussion we see from the words which our Saviour immediately subjoins: "Simon, Simon, behold, Satan asked to have you, that he might sift you as wheat." Peter and the other Apostles did not yield to the temptation, but the Popes did. They attempted to appropriate to themselves all the power of the Church, and vied with the emperors in pomp and influence, entirely forgetting that "the kingdom of God cometh not with observation," *i.e.*, "with splendour and outward show" (St. Luke xvii. 20). However the Church was too narrow a field for their greediness; they saw the world that it was beautiful and desirable, and they stretched their hands out and took of the forbidden fruit. Our Saviour warned them saying: "My kingdom is not of this world." But His voice was like "the voice of one crying in the wilderness." The Devil, however, took the proud Pontiffs up into an exceeding high mountain, and showed them all the kingdoms of the world, and the glory of them; and said unto them, "All these things will I give you, if you will fall down and worship me." And they fell down and worshipped him. And the *Pope-king* became mighty among the kings of the world, emperors trembled before him, held his stirrup when he mounted, and stood barefooted, shivering, clad in sackcloth in his courtyard. The thunderbolts of *Jupiter Tonans* were never so much feared as the thunders of the Vatican. The Pope enthroned and dethroned kings and emperors and distributed the globe. In fact, the Pope became the master of the world, *as the Devil "the prince of this world" had promised him.* And the Pope-king, forgetting that "the foxes have holes, and the birds of the heaven have nests, but the Son of Man had not where to lay His head," built for himself a house, a palace, *the grandest palace of the world.* It covers a large space, and is 1151 feet long, 767 feet broad. It contains 4422 chambers, and has eight grand staircases (including the *scala regia*), and 200 smaller ones, and twenty courts. This is the "Apostolic" dwelling of "the successor of St. Peter." The Patriarch of Constantinople lives in an unsightly wooden house, is poor, and lives as a poor man; his daily fare is simple in the extreme, yet his hospitality marvellous, as we know from personal experience.

The Popes had, in course of time, in consequence of legacies and donations, acquired an immense landed property, but they were, after all, but the first subjects of the Byzantine emperor. Rankling envy stirred the Popes up to look about for a tool able to conquer for them the long-wished-for indedependence and political sovereignty. A fine opportunity offered itself. The *legitimate* but weak king Childeric III. was dethroned by his ambitious Prime-Minister (*major domus*) Pepin, and, wishing to legitimate his usurpation, the latter applied to Pope Zacharias, who readily complied with his request, on a ground *which every ambitious Prime-Minister of the present day may appeal to in order to overturn his weak king and usurp his crown.* Thus the preparing step for Papal sovereignty was a REVOLUTIONARY ACT of Papacy, and shows what a big lie it is when the Popes declare themselves to be *the mainstay of legitimacy*, *the prop of conservatism.* They were revolutionists from the beginning, and will continue so to the end. They are in worldly affairs democrats of the purest water, as Bellarmine (*De Rom. Pontiff.* i. 6) informs us, saying that the Church's power is not like "the civil power, which is vested in the people, unless it be transferred by the people to a prince" (*civili potestati quæ est in populo, nisi a populo transferatur in principem*). Thus Bellarmine, though hating and vilifying democracy in the whole chapter, still admits it as a civil principle. Wherever there was a fortunate adventurer breaking his solemn oath in order to become an emperor, the Pope blessed him and courted him. As soon as Don Carlos and the Count de Chambord reminded the Pope of the principles of Legitimacy, he turned the cold shoulder on them. Not *Legitimacy* but *Expediency* is Rome's principle. Let the Nihilists restore to the Pope his lost States, and let them place on the throne of Russia an Ultramontane Prince, and the Pope will grant them a plenary indulgence, and give them his blessing into the bargain. In Prussia the Ultramontanes fraternise with the Social Democrats; in Poland they systematically oppose the Russian Government; in Ireland they do very much the same opposite the English Government, though it was Pope Hadrian IV. (Nicholas Breakspear, the only Englishman who ever ascended the Papal throne) who presented Ireland (which did not belong to him) to King Henry II. of England, or rather gave him leave to conquer it, as Pope Gregory VII., the friend of

William the Conqueror, acquiesced in the invasion of England by the latter. Indeed splendid instances of the Pope's *upholding legitimacy!* Pepin was king, but the Longobards oppressed Pope Stephen II., who went to France and anointed Pepin and his sons, in recompense of which Pepin had to sign a document by which he engaged himself to conquer the Exarchate, which the Longobards had wrested from the hands of the Byzantine Emperor, and to hand it over to the Pope. Pepin accomplished the conquest. When the Emperor sent his Legates *to reclaim his lawful property*, Pepin referred to the Pope as *owner.* In private life we should call such transactions *cheat and robbery*, but as part and parcel of the "Patrimonium S. Petri" they are hallowed. Or shall we defend *main force* as a "legal title," and cover the robberies of the Longobards with a moral cloak? Then we might as well all at once sanction highway robbery. This is the *totally immoral* basis of the Papal States, which God's just retribution has destroyed in our days, but to which the blind Popes still cling as to the last plank of their shipwreck.

Shall we recount all the subsequent struggles of the Popes for the extension of their territory, the deluge of blood shed for the acquisition of land, the sieges and pillaging of towns, the horrors of famine and pestilence attending the wars, the excommunications and interdicts used as political weapons? *God has judged!* The Pontifical States are swept away for ever, only a long track of blood and ruin they have left behind on the pages of history as a mark of their infernal origin and a warning to the present and future generations to come out of Babylon.

From the preceding we see that the Western Church had already advanced a good deal in the wrong way before it formally separated from the East. Yet the dogmas were still the same in both Churches, and the Western alterations in the fundamental Church constitution were not yet dogmatically fixed. The East exercised always a wholesome check on Western arbitrariness and greed of power. Now, since the bond in 1054 was severed, the Western passions went rapidly down-hill. The bitter fruits of Schism soon showed themselves. And the finger of God is not less visible in preserving the Eastern Church in its pure ancient Orthodoxy than it is in allowing the West to follow its own vain conceits. Being cut off from the true Church, the abode of the Holy Ghost, means shifting for one's self. Hence the supremely human *development* of the Roman system in doctrine and discipline. It is ridiculous to hear the Romans claim *perpetuity of faith*, as half a dozen of new dogmas have sprung up since they separated from the East, and Heaven knows how many more will follow in future. Must not common sense admit that *what was Catholic at the time of the seventh Œcumenical Council must be Catholic now, and must be so for ever?* We are now what the Romans were at the time of the seventh Œcumenical Council, and what they *then* believed to be Catholic. *Now* this belief is by them considered antiquated, defective, or altogether wrong, as their present belief will perhaps be considered in the next century. Is that St. Vincent of Lerin's rule of faith? "What always, everywhere, and by all has been believed" (*quod semper, ubique, et ab omnibus creditum est*)?

Scarcely the schism was accomplished when Pope Nicholas II. (1059) deprived the clergy and people of Rome of the right to elect their Bishop, and, without any ceremony, conferred it on the College of Cardinals. Now the system of concentrating, securing, and developing the Pope's ecclesiastical and secular power began to work in good earnest. Now the *Curia Romana,* the most complicated politico-ecclesiastical machinery, began to be formed. The consciences were no longer *morally*, but *juridically*, to be treated. A tariff of the most oppressive taxes for all sorts of spiritual needs was introduced; favour and bribery were flourishing. Witchcraft was invented, witches burnt, their property confiscated. Coercive power was usurped by the Papal Church, contrary to Christ's command; heretics and schismatics, personal and political enemies, were tortured and burnt or executed. The Inquisition with its horrors sprang up. And Rome, not content with such enormities, even canonised these unchristian principles by raising to the rank of saints two monsters in human form, viz., the blood-stained Grand-Inquisitor Arbues, and the furious grave-desecrator Josaphat

Kunciewicz, who could not leave in peace the very bones and ashes of the Orthodox dead. Heathen Greece would have condemned him, but Christian Rome beatified him! "Ye shall know them by their fruits."

Quite different is the aspect of the Orthodox Church. She does not know of witches, of Inquisition, of scapularies, of indulgences, of dispensations, with their concomitant taxes, of *casus reservati* (sins from which the Pope only can absolve), of the *quinquennalia* (rights granted by the Pope to the Bishops, which lapse if not renewed every five years), of the *altaria privilegiata* (altars on which every Mass said delivers a soul from Purgatory). She does not claim *coercive power*, but most emphatically condemns it. Her weapons are only spiritual; she leaves bodily punishment to God. She has not forgotten St. Luke ix. 54–56: "When His disciples James and John saw this, they said, Lord, wilt Thou that we command fire to come down from heaven, and consume them, even as Elias did? But He turned and *rebuked* them, and said, *Ye know not what manner of spirit ye are of.* For the Son of Man *is not come to destroy men's lives*, but to save them." And again said Jesus to Peter (St. Matt. xxvi. 52): "Put up again thy sword in its place: for all they that take the sword shall perish with the sword." Peter, obedient to his Master's command, put up again his sword into its place, but "Peter's successors" *did not;* they took the sword, waged war, shed blood in torrents, conquered one place after another, lost one place after another, till the Cross of Savoy came down upon them, and *they perished with the sword.* It is a curious, not to say providential, fact that Piedmont, the first country touched by Pepin on his invading tour in Italy, when Pope Stephen asked him *to take the sword in St. Peter's behalf*, was the very country that was to destroy the Papal States.

The ancient Church did not hold these principles of the later Roman Church, nor did the Orthodox Church hold them at any time. Tertullian in his treatise on "Patience" (chap. iii.) says: "He to whom, had he willed it, legions of angels would at one word have presented themselves from the heavens, *approved not the avenging sword of even one disciple.*

The patience of the Lord was wounded in [the person of] Malchus. And so, too, *He cursed for the time to come the works of the sword.*" Again, in his work against Marcion (iv. 2, 3), after having quoted Isaiah xlii. 2, 3 ("A bruised reed shall He not crush, and smoking flax shall He not quench"), he adds: "Being of such a character, He was of course much the less disposed *to burn men.* For even at that time the Lord said to Elias He was not in the fire, but in the still small voice." The Romans have constantly in their mouth the beautiful saying, "The Church does not thirst for blood" (*ecclesia not sitit sanguinem*), but hecatombs of victims give them the lie, whereas the Orthodox Church in her practice has always adhered to this principle. Socrates (Hist. Eccl. vii. 3) says: "It is not a custom with the Orthodox Church to persecute" (*οὐκ εἰωθὸς διώκειν τῇ ὀρθοδόξῳ ἐκκλησίᾳ*). And St. Athanasius (Hist. Arian. ad Monach. n. 67, Migne xxv. p. 773), "It is a characteristic of religion *not to force but to persuade*" (*θεοσεβείας ἴδιον μὴ ἀναγκάζειν, ἀλλὰ πείθειν*). Lactantius (Institut. Div. v. 19, in other editions 20), "*Religion cannot be imposed by force;* the matter must be carried on *by words rather than by blows,* that the will may be affected. Let them unsheath the weapon of their intellect; if their system is true, let it be asserted. We are prepared to hear, if they teach; while they are silent, we certainly pay no credit to them, as we do not yield to them even in their rage. Let them imitate us in setting forth the system of the whole matter, for we do not entice, as they say, but *we teach, we prove, we show.* And thus *no one is detained by us against his will, for he is unserviceable to God who is destitute of faith and devotedness;* and yet no one departs from us, since the truth itself detains him. Let them teach in this manner, if they have any confidence in the truth; let them speak, let them give utterance; let them venture, I say, to discuss with us something of this nature; and then assuredly their error and folly will be ridiculed by the old women, whom they despise, and by our boys." * St. John Chrysostom (Hom. 46 in

---

* *Religio cogi non potest. Verbis potius quam verberibus* res agenda est, ut sit

Matth. n. 1, 2, Migne, Patres Graeci, tom. lviii. p. 447) teaches expressly that the Lord forbids to kill heretics. Augustine (Contra literas Petiliani, ii. 83) says: "Nobody is to be constrained to accept the faith against his will (*ad fidem nullus est cogendus invitus*). Cassiodorus (end of the fifth century) says (Varia. Epist. ii. 27): "We cannot command religion, because nobody is compelled to believe against his will" (*religionem imperare non possumus, quia nemo cogitur, ut credat invitus*). Theodore Studita (826) was one of the fiercest enemies of religious persecution, and maintained that heretics were to be advised but not to be killed (lib. ii. epist. 155). The Byzantine emperors did, indeed, not act according to the principles of their Church in persecuting and punishing the Manicheans, Paulicians, and Bogomils, and confiscating their property, but they were neither instigated nor backed by their Church. It was not an Orthodox, but the Monophysite Empress Theodora, who is said to have killed 100,000 Paulicians. It is, however, fair to add that the said sects were persecuted chiefly for their gross *immorality*, which emperors can and must remove. When Patriarch Nicephorus tried to associate with the Emperor Michael I. in this bloody business, the indignation of the clergy compelled him not to do so. It is not proved that the Patriarch John IV. Nesteutes (the Faster) was a privy to the execution of Paulinus; Theodore Studita believes that he is not. Maximus, Patriarch of Constantinople, wrote in 1480 to Giovanni Mocenigo, Doge of Venice, "that the law of God does not admit of constraint" (*νόμον Θεοῦ τὸ ἀβίαστον*). And in the Council convened in the Church of Hagia Sophia at Constantinople for the purpose of rejecting the Council of Florence, the Bishops solemnly *condemned any restraint in matters of religion.* Metrophanes Critopulos,

---

voluntas. Distringant aciem ingeniorum suorum. Si ratio eorum vera est, asseratur (*alii:* afferatur). Parati sumus audire, si doceant; tacentibus certe nihil credimus; sicut ne sævientibus quidem cedimus. Imitentur nos, aut rationem rei exponant. Nos enim non illicimus, ut ipsi objectant, sed *docemus, probamus, ostendimus. Itaque nemo a nobis retinetur invitus. Inutilis est enim Deo, qui devotione ac fide caret.* Et tamen nemo discedit, ipsa veritate retinente. Doceant isti hoc modo, si qua illis fiducia veritatis est; loquantur, hiscant; audeant, inquam, disputare nobiscum aliquid ejusmodi, jam profecto ab aniculis, quas contemnunt, et a pueris nostratibus error illorum ac stultitia irridebitur.

Patriarch of Alexandria (sixteenth century), in his Confessio (cap. vii.), states it as a mark of the true Church "that she persecutes nobody, but rather suffers persecution from all, and never yields to persecutions, but always firmly resists them, and by divine power prevails on the persecutors." * The practice of the Latins was the very reverse, so that the highly Ultramontane Pope Innocent III., a decided enemy of the Greek Church, wrote in 1205, in a letter to Boniface of Montferrat (De Bréquigny, Epist. Innoc. III., lib. viii. ep. 133, tom ii. p. 769), about the Greek Church, "which saw in the Latins only examples of reprobates and works of darkness, so that *she justly abhors them more than dogs*" (*quæ in Latinis non nisi perditionis exempla et opera tenebrarum aspexit, ut jam merito illos abhorreat plus quam canes*). But let the reader peruse our article, "Hagia Sophia in Constantinople and London" (*Orthodox Catholic Review*, vol. viii. pp. 191–208), giving a detailed account taken from contemporary historians, and his hair will stand on end. However, such were but the natural fruits of the Roman principles.

Schism almost invariably leads to *heresy*. In 1215 Papal Supremacy was declared a dogma, and based on a divine right. As this question had been the fundamental cause of the schism, it was but natural that it should be first secured. But in doing so the Romans had inflicted on themselves an irreparable evil—had burned the ships behind them, so that a return to Orthodoxy is impossible, unless they declare themselves heretics, and repentingly retrace their steps. In 1439 the Filioque became a dogma. For further information, let us refer to our treatise, "The Bonn Conferences and the Filioque Question" (*Orthodox Catholic Review*, vol. iv. pp. 217–264). In 1854 the Immaculate Conception of the Holy Virgin became a dogma—a dogma without even a show of traditional basis, a speculative product of mistaken devotion, a pet opinion of Pius IX.—the first dogma proclaimed by a

---

* Τὸ *μηδένας μὲν ταύτην διώκειν, διώκεσθας δὲ ὑπὸ πάντων καὶ μηδέποτε τοῖς διωγμοῖς ἐνδιδόναι, ἀλλ' ἀνενδότως τούτοις ἀεὶ ἀνθίστασθαι καὶ θείᾳ δυνάμει τῶν διωκόντων περιγίγνεσθαι* (Kimmel, Append. p. 104). Compare the interesting Essay (*Δοκίμιον*) on Critopulos by our late friend Archimandrite Dr. A. Demetrakopulos, Leipzig, 1870.

Pope superseding the authority of the voice of a General Council. In 1870 we saw the crowning of the schismatico-heretical edifice by the dogma of the Papal Infallibility, anticipated already in the mode of proclaiming the former dogma. People commonly think that here the *circulus vitiosus* is at an end, but they are greatly mistaken. Papal Infallibility will prove the starting-point of a new development of dogmas, the possibility of which the present Infallibilists will deny and ridicule as they denied and ridiculed Papal Infallibility before it was cut out and ready-made for their acceptance. Our present Infallibilists screen themselves behind the elastic term *ex cathedra*, which Cardinal Manning and Bishop Hefele scarcely understand in the same sense. Clever lies have generally a Protean face, change with one's position and eye-glasses, have a dash of truth in themselves, and only require a dexterous handling to appear remarkably lifelike. Hear a gentle persuasive Roman, and he will represent the new doctrine as a harmless dogma, since the condition "*ex cathedra*" is a matter of doubt and dispute. But we do not believe that the Pope has simply played a comedy. "Why then not give us rather a list of those Papal Bulls, or parts of Bulls, and other Papal utterings which are to be accepted as infallible?" the reader will object. Our answer is: This would be too restrictive and limited; the Pope will have the whole field to himself, will not be controlled by anybody; will have your signature under a blank in order to be able to fill the blank space with whatever he likes. The Pope is too much of a diplomate not to know that one must not bend too much the bow. Therefore he allows his theologians to fight with each other, and waits for the right moment, *i.e.*, when the more advanced Papal party has gained a signal victory, to push forward. Be sure the Jesuits are heartily glad that loquacious Pius is gone. Father Curci has told us as much in his new book, and Father Curci is still a full-blown Jesuit, though, for decency's sake, an ex-Jesuit. Now, to a single-hearted, pious, and straightforward Catholic this whole affair must look very much like humbug. The old Church defined dogmas, and the people knew what to believe. And if new disputes rose, a new Council cleared the clouds away. But this odern dogma was from the first moment unintelligible, nd everybody understood it as he liked, just as the Pro-stant understands his Bible. I doubt whether there are wo persons in the whole Roman Church, the infallible Pope cluded, who understand the dogma in the same way. Of ourse we mean two persons who really care to get at the eaning, for there are millions of Roman Catholics who ither do not care a pin's head for the new imposition, or stolidly repeat the words of their priests like a parrot. The gloomy picture grows still gloomier when you think what this dogma, this mysterious object, may include. The poisonous seed is sown, what may the plant, the full-grown plant be? We do not indulge in fancies or un-substantial apprehensions. However, things do sometimes ast their shadows before them. In the Council of Trent the modern dogma of the Immaculate Conception was mooted and foreshadowed. Let us look for other shadows of things that are sure to come. We do not mean trifles, as, *e.g.*, the probable future dogma of the bodily assumption of the Holy Virgin, or perhaps (but not very likely) the extension of the Immaculate Conception to Mary's parents. But we mean the development of the Infallibility dogma, which is the pivot of all wishes and studies of the Roman Pontiffs. This is the battlefield of the future, the pleasure-ground of the present.

We meet with one of these ominous and portentous shadows in the speech of James Lainez delivered in the Council of Trent on the 20th of October 1562. Lainez was the companion and bosom-friend of Ignatius of Loyola, the founder of the Society of Jesus, and his successor as General of the Order. As the characteristic feature of Papacy is fully developed in the organisation of this Order, and as its members add to the common monastic vows that of implicit obedience to the Pope, it was but natural that the Jesuits considered themselves the privileged guardians and developers of the Papal idea. The Jesuits were the most obedient sons of the Pope *as long as he obeyed them.* When the Pope was recalcitrant and unmanageable, they fled to seek shelter under the protecting wings of "*schismatic*" *Russia and* "*heretic*" *Prussia*, till the Pope repented and called them back. So it was, in fact, "the black Pope" (*il papa nero*, the General of the Jesuits), and not "the white Pope" (*il papa bianco*), who governed the Church, and we have to seek in the shrine of the hearts of the Jesuit leaders for the key to the mystery of the Roman Sphinx. Jesuits are very clever and diplomatically reticent, but they are after all men, and so it happens on rare occasions that they are injudiciously open, and betray secrets far in advance of the right moment. Such was the case with Lainez's speech. It so disconcerted and frightened the Fathers of the Council that Lainez was forbidden to publish it. However, the tenor of the speech was transmitted to us by two very different men, Pauli Sarpi (writing under the pseudonym of Soave), a clever but frivolous man, hating Rome with all the hatred of a true Venetian patriot; and Sforza Pallavicini, an equally clever man, learned and respected, but fanatic and blinded by his Jesuit prejudices, loving Papacy with all the love of an infatuated suitor. Combining or comparing both, we generally approach the truth as confirmed by other documents. In one respect Sarpi deserves the preference, because he was a contemporary, a boy of ten years, when the speech was delivered, whereas Pallavicini was born only in 1607, and could therefore scarcely consult ear-witnesses, as Sarpi could. Notwithstanding, we prefer quoting Pallavicini, because he is a favourite with the Romans, and his testimony will therefore fully be admitted. We quote from the best edition, "*Istoria del Concilio di Trento scritta dal padre Sforza Pallavicini*" (with notes by Zaccaria), Romæ, 1833. In spite of Pallavicini's invectives against Sarpi (Soave), we find both accounts of Lainez's speech very much the same, except when Sarpi adds some dashes of sarcastic wit, *e.g.*, he makes Lainez say that our Lord said to Peter, "Tend My sheep," because the sheep was the most patient of all animals. But these bad wits are easily discernible. Pallavicini found the speech (or at least a rough copy of it) by accident in the Vatican archives, bound up with some other documents. Lainez prefaced the subject by saying that "many had dissuaded him from undertaking this work, *lest he might incur the blame of being a flatterer of the Pope.*" * Then he divides his speech into four parts—(1) laying down the question; (2) stating his own view; (3) refuting the opposite party; and (4) proving his own view with arguments. However, the whole speech is nothing but an exposition of his own view and a condemnation of the opposite one. In n. 6, p. 770, he (Lainez) "maintained that the power of the Episcopal order is from God directly in all individuals, but that the power of jurisdiction was from God directly *in genere, i.e.*, in some, as in Peter and his successors, and, according to his opinion, also in all the Apostles by a special privilege; *in the others, as in the particular Bishops*, this power emanated, by a medium interposed by God, *directly from the Pope.*" † And in n. 11, p. 773: "It was certain that He (Christ) wished the Bishops should possess jurisdiction, but *not as such that was given them directly by Him.*" ‡ And in n. 12, Lainez ventures even the hazardous assertion that "many Fathers" had "expressly taught" that "the jurisdiction of the Bishops was from the Pope" (*che la jurisdizione sia dal papa*). And in n. 14, p. 775, he adds that "the decisions of the Councils were decisions of God, *as far as they issue from the Pope, who is assisted by the Holy Ghost.*" § Thus all difference between Œcumenical and Particular Councils, emphatically taught by the Undivided Church, has disappeared. Yea, the Councils on the whole are superseded, since the Pope alone enjoys the assistance of the Holy Ghost. *Then* the Fathers of the Council were frightened at such bold and sweeping assertions; *now* these assertions are sanctioned by the Vatican

---

* Pallav. Istor. del. Conc. di Trento, tom. iii. lib. xviii. cap. 15, n. 2, p. 768: "Molti l'aveano disconfortato da quell' opera, acciocchè non cadesse in biasimo d'adulatore verso il pontefice."

† "Affermò, che la podestà dell' ordine episcopale è da Dio immediatamente in tutti gl' individui: quella della giurisdizione essere da Dio immediatamente in genere, cioè in alcuni, come in Pietro e ne' successori, e, secondo ch' egli teneva, ancora in tutti gli apostoli per ispecial privilegio: *negli altri, come ne' vescovi particolari*, proceder essa, per interposito mezzo da Dio, *immediatamente dal papa.*"

‡ "Certo essere, che volle ne' vescovi la giurisdizione, *ma non data loro immediatamente da se.*"

§ "Le decisioni de' Concilj esser decisioni di Dio *in quanto sono dal papa, a cui lo Spirito Santo assiste.*"

Council, the Bishops are degraded to the rank of Papal delegates, and the Pope has become "Episcopus episcoporum," a title once derided by Tertullian, and "Episcopus universalis," a title condemned by Pope St. Gregory the Great.

But Lainez's speech goes beyond the decrees of the Vatican Council, and affords us a peep into the distance. He grants, indeed, that the power conferred by the ordination is directly from God. But what he gives with one hand, he takes away with the other; for what is the use of having a thing if I may not use it *except by permission of the Pope*, who can thus frustrate the gift of God? Therefore the Sacrament of Order, though *theoretically* the gift of the Holy Ghost, is *virtually* the gift of the Pope. And the words of Lainez (as reported by Sarpi) are quite consistent with the rest of his speech: "Let them (the Fathers) take care lest, *by wishing to make the institution of Bishops one of divine right*, they destroy the hierarchy." * Cardinal Cajetan speaks still more explicitly: "He set Peter up, . . . from whom, in the ordinary way, all should derive the power of jurisdiction *and of order*." † Silvester Prierias (*In præsumptuosas M. Lutheri conclusiones de potestate papæ dialogus*, Lipsiæ, 1518, p. 2) says: "Whoever does not rest upon the doctrine of the Roman Church *and of the Roman Pope* as on *the infallible rule of faith*, from which (doctrine) also the Holy Scripture derives its strength and authority, is a heretic." And again (apud *Roccabert.* tom. xix. 2356): "The Apostle Peter *alone* has been directly appointed a Bishop by Christ." And on the same page: "It is by Peter that all Apostles have been ordained Bishops." And again on the next page he maintains that THE POPE IS VIRTUALLY THE CATHOLIC CHURCH, THE HEAD OF THE WORLD, AND VIRTUALLY THE

* Hist. Conc. Trident., Lipsiæ, p. 1054: "Videant ne, *dum episcoporum institutionem juris divini facere volunt*, hierarchiam tollant."

† Cajetan apud Roccabertum, "*Bibliotheca Maxima Pontificia*," Romæ, 1699, tom. xix. 449: "Posuit Petrum . . . a quo in omnes potestas jurisdictionis et *ordinis* ordinarie derivaretur." This *Bibl. Max. Pont.* was compiled by Roccaberti, Archbishop of Valentia, in twenty-one volumes in folio (1695–99), dedicated to Pope Innocent XII. Every volume bears the *Imprimatur*, sanctioning the principles proposed in the same.

WHOLE WORLD.* Reader, remember that the Pope's *Imprimatur* has sanctioned this sentence! But though the Roman Catholic is hereby not compelled to adopt the views proposed, still he is bound to admit that the views proposed *may safely be held, since they do not contain any heresy, nor do even smack of heresy* (*hæresin sapiens*). This is the cautious manner how Rome prepares the way for smuggling in new material for the dogmatic manufactory. First, books are written in which the new view is proposed, timidly and covertly, in order to feel the pulse of public opinion. Contradiction opens the skirmish, and the question is more fully and more freely ventilated. The dimensions of the party strife increase, the age and strength of the baby-doctrine grow apace, and the Pope may safely step forward from his hiding-place and show his colour, not indeed as a decided partisan (that would be unwise and might damage his cause), but by some *imprimatur*. This is the *theoretical* stage of the controversy. Then the *practical* begins by coining devotional books to introduce the future doctrine into the minds of the faithful and to mix it up with the life-blood of the poor, unwary souls. This is *the most infernal part* of the business, poisoning the blood, and killing innocent people by inches. Now the *Tradition* is ready; the people have been trained to look upon the matter as inherited from time immemorial. Only one link is wanting. It is Catholic doctrine that every dogma must be proved to be part of the *Apostolic* deposit of faith. Now it is remarkably difficult to trace the modern dogmas back to the Apostles, since we know on the whole the date when every new dogma was born and named, and the place where the cradles of the infants stood. In the face of these public facts a pedigree is forged reaching to the Apostles, a pedigree without names, without proofs, without documents. This pedigree is supplied by the *latent* or *dormant* tradition. This prodigious assumption reasons in this way: "If St. Gregory, Leo, Augustine, Jerome, Chrysostom, Basil, Cyprian, Ignatius, the Apostles

* "Quia adversarius (Lutherus) negat, *eum* (Papam) *esse ecclesiam catholicam virtualiter*, eapropter ostendendum est, quod sit *caput orbis*, et consequenter *orbis totus in virtute*."

John, James, Paul, Peter would hear our dogma, they would at once recognise it as their own; but as they had no opportunity of stating and defending what was not attacked at their time, express proofs are wanting." He who can acquiesce in such a reasoning is capable of gulping down any nonsense. St. Peter (1 Pet. ii. 2) taught very differently that we should long for *reasonable* food *which is without guile* (τὸ λογικὸν ἄδολον γάλα). The hypothesis of a *latent* tradition is the most insidious snare of Romanism. Of course an upright and thinking outsider will not so easily fall into it; but a person born and bred a Roman does not find the *sacrifizio d'intelletto** so difficult, but rather delightfully easy. People like others to think for them and care for them, provided these guides are lenient and do not encroach on the comforts of life.

History was always the weak point of the Jesuits, and consequently of the Papists. If this nasty and troublesome stumbling-block could be cleared away altogether, Romanism would be *irrefutable.* But it is with history as with conscience. Could the criminal only clear away his provokingly uncomfortable conscience, he would be a perfectly happy man. *History is the conscience of mankind*, and Rome by falsifying it has sealed her own doom.

It is interesting to hear from Silvester Prierias that Peter ordained the other Apostles Bishops.† But whence has he

* There is an interesting book, "*Epistolæ præpositorum generalium ad superiores Societatis Jesu*" (Dilingæ, 1612). The book opens with a letter of the General Everard Mercurianus, followed by six letters of the General Claudius Aquaviva, all inculcating the duty of blind obedience. Then follows a second part without a separate title, but with a new pagination, containing a selection of letters of the Generals of the Society made in 1606 by Bernard de Angelis. This part begins with a letter of Ignatius of Loyola, founder of the Society, "*de obedientiæ virtute.*" In this letter we read, p. 8 : "He who will entirely immolate himself to God must, beside the will, also *sacrifice his intellect*, which is the third and highest degree of obedience" (*qui vero se totum penitus immolare vult Deo, præter voluntatem intelligentiam quoque, qui tertius et summus est gradus obedientiæ, offerat necesse est*). And p. 17 : As you directly assent to the Catholic truth, "so set to work to execute whatever the Superior says *with a blind impetus of a will intent on obeying, without any inquiry whatever*" (. . . *sic ad ea facienda, quæcunque Superior dixerit, cæco quodam impetu voluntatis parendi cupidæ, sine ulla prorsus disquisitione feramini*). This is the principle of the people of whom Cervantes says : "As guides and leaders on the way to heaven few come up to them" (*para guiadores y adalides del camino del cielo pocos les llegan*), Novelas ejemplares (los dos perros).

† Bellarmine (Opp. Colon. 1620, tom. ii. 274) is still better informed. He says

gathered this piece of information? History does not know of it. A special divine revelation Prierias did not claim. How did he then get the news? Simply by argument. He may have argued somewhat in this way: "The Pope is undoubtedly the infallible teacher and supreme master of the Church, consequently Peter held the same position among the Apostles, which would not have been the case if he had not ordained the others; *ergo* Peter *must* have ordained them." So history is manufactured from supposed dogmas. Would it not have been safer to argue: "Since history does not bear out my theory, it falls to the ground"? Goldwin Smith ("Lectures on the Study of History," Oxford, 1861, p. 25) very appositely remarks: "'Truth does not regard consequences' was a noble saying; but there are some cases in which the consequences are *a test of truth.*"

Papal Infallibility has perplexed and unsettled the minds of many serious Roman Catholics who cannot ignore the fatal dilemma, the contradiction between history and modern dogma. As to the unthinking mass, Hosea Biglow is right:—

> "A merciful Providence fashioned them hollow
> On purpose that they might their principles swallow."

However, Papal Infallibility is only the bud of a mysterious fruit, the development of which will bring to light startling results, foreshadowed by mediæval writers from the fourteenth century downwards. Alvaro Pelayo (apud *Roccabert.* iii. 52, 2) says: "What the Pope does God does" (*quod papa facit*

---

that Peter alone was ordained Bishop by Christ, James and John by Peter, and the rest of the Apostles by these three. Was perhaps the Canon that a Bishop is to be ordained by three Bishops then already in force? At all events, the Romans seem to admit not only "doctrinal" but also "historical" *development.* Thus we may expect to see the *revision of the Catechism* in course of time followed by a *revision of Gospel and Church history*, somewhat more in accordance with the tenets of the Papal Church. Why should the Roman not read in the Gospel (St. John xv. 26): ". . . the Spirit of Truth, which proceedeth from the Father *and me,*" since he says that this is the full truth? There is nothing in the context to forbid this reading, and as Christ *must* have foreseen that the present text is *misleading*, intrinsic reasons compel the consistent Roman to suppose that the original text *must* have been "from the Father *and me.*" The Romans are still too timid to enter upon this line of revision and reconstruction, but will it not be in the end their inevitable lot?

Deus facit). Cardinal Jacobatius (ix. 516, 77) says: "The Pope *can say and do whatever he likes*, provided it is not against the faith, from which there is no dispensation."* The exception is ridiculous, for is it not the Pope who infallibly declares what the Catholic faith is? The same author says in another place: "The Pope and Christ constitute the same consistory, so that, with the exception of sin, *the Pope can do almost everything that God can.*"† Bellarmine affirms that the Pope possesses *the supreme power in temporal affairs by divine right*, though not directly, yet indirectly. This did not satisfy Pope Sixtus V., as he claimed this as a direct right, and he placed the book on the Index. The Jesuit Gregory de Valentia (apud *Roccabert.* xiii. 141, 2) says: "Whether the Pope carefully studies the matter to be decided or not, if he only decides the controversy, he will decide it certainly infallibly."‡ Pope Sixtus V., Domin. Gravina, Duval, Michael Maucler, Gregory de Valentia, &c., extend the prerogative of Infallibility to the canonisation of saints. The Decretum Gratiani (ed. Migne, 1861, p. 1324) says: "The Holy Roman Church [or the Pope, which is at present identical] imparts right and authority to the Holy Canons, *but is not bound by them.* It so lends authority to the Canons that *it does not subject itself to them.*" § Has Gratian (or rather the Pope) read St. Matt. xxiii. 4? "They bind heavy burdens and grievous to be borne, and lay them on men's shoulders; but *they themselves will not move them with their finger.*" The Popes St. Leo the Great, Agatho, and Gregory the Great were of a different opinion.

We showed the rapid decline and change in the Roman Church since it separated from the East, which had hitherto been a check and curb to the Western innovating proclivities.

* "Dummodo contra fidem non veniat, contra quam nulla est dispensatio (papa) *potest dicere et facere, quidquid ei placet.*"

† "Papa et Christus faciunt idem consistorium, ita quod excepto peccato *potest papa fere omnia facere quod potest Deus.*"

‡ "Sive Pontifex in definiendo studium adhibeat, sive non adhibeat, modo tamen controversiam definiat, infallibiliter certe definiet."

§ "Sacrosancta Romana ecclesia jus et auctoritatem sanctis canonibus impertitur, *sed non eis alligatur.* Ita canonibus auctoritatem præstat, *ut se ipsam non subjiciat eis.*"

Now it was unfettered and free, as the prodigal son was when he left his home. Dogmas were coined; a Canon Law of absolutism and chains of slavery forged; an oppressive system of taxation introduced; superstitions fostered and developed. Meanwhile the ferment of innovation spread; not one of the Seven Sacraments was left intact, as we have shown in our Latin book "*Libellus Invitatorius ad Clerum Laicosque Romano-Catholicos, qui antiquam Occidentis Ecclesiam Catholicam ad pristinam puritatem et gloriam restauratam videre cupiunt* (Halle, 1871). Let the reader be so good as to consult this book for the details and references of the next pages.

The way of making the *Sign of the Cross* was up to the middle of the fifteenth century the same in East and West, *i.e.*, the same as the Orthodox Church has preserved it until the present day. Pope Innocent III. writes (1198) that this is the proper mode of making it. The present Roman way of making it seems to be copied from the *Monophysites*, according to the description given by the Nestorian Metropolitan, Elias of Damascus (893), in his Arabic Nomocanon (Assemani Biblioth. Oriental. tom. iii. par. i. p. 515). Thus the schism was marked by the change of the most ancient *badge of Catholicity.*

I. *Baptism.*—The *trine immersion* was an Apostolic tradition, and adhered to in East and West up to the twelfth century. In Britain and Ireland it was most conscientiously observed. The Council of Cashel (1171) strictly enjoins it.

II. *Confirmation.*—The Jesuit Perrone affirms (after Martene) that for the first twelve centuries Baptism and Confirmation were combined, as it is in the Orthodox Church, and as was the case in the British Church (as Howel states). In the Gallican Church this custom was still later in use. Now, since the baptizing minister, as a rule, is a priest, Confirmation was administered by priests, as it is in the Orthodox Church, and was not reserved to Bishops, as it now is in the Roman and in the Anglican Church. St. Ambrose, Jerome, Chrysostom, and other Fathers recognise the priest as minister of this Sacrament, but the Popes Innocent III. and Gregory IX. declared the Confirmation by a priest to be *invalid*, and introduced the sacrilegious habit of *reconfirming*, strongly disapproved by Abraham Ecchellensis and Cardinal Bona (*Analecta Liturgico-sacra*, p. 363, 18). Where is here the Papal Infallibility? Or is it not a dogmatic declaration, if the decision concerns the *validity of a Sacrament?* Moreover, mark the great inconsistency: up to the great schism, Rome did not hesitate to recognise the Confirmations by Greek priests as *valid!*

III. *Holy Eucharist.*—This Sacrament is quite disfigured by Roman innovations. (1.) The Romans set aside the solemn injunction of our Lord: "Drink ye *all* of it," depriving the communicants of the cup, which only the celebrant partakes of. If the injunction of Christ solely concerned the Apostles and their successors, the Bishops and priests (as the Romans say), how is it that up to the twelfth century (as Bona has proved), both the clergy and laity in the West as well as in the East received the Communion under both kinds, and after that time "the use of the chalice grew *obsolete*"? The Orthodox Church agrees in this with Pope Gelasius, who says that "the division of one and the same Sacrament cannot take place *without a great sacrilege.*" (2.) The Romans have abolished *Infant-Communion*, which was observed by the whole Church during the first eight centuries. St. Cyprian, Augustine, Pope Innocent, Gennadius, &c., highly commend and praise it. It is only the spirit of Rationalism inherent in innovating Papism that has reserved Communion and Confirmation to the time *when the children are able to understand what they receive*, just as if baptized infants have no life of grace working in them. But life (*gratia infusa*) requires *food* and *strength.* The Romans, according to this their Rationalistic principle, ought to have begun by postponing Baptism to a later period of life. (3.) The bread used for the Holy Eucharist was taken from the loaves which the faithful took with them to church as an oblation. This was their common daily bread, consequently *leavened.* Before the ninth century we have no proof that *unleavened bread* was used in the Eucharist. This bread has again in course of time degenerated into a mere *wafer*, which scarcely can be called *food.* The Jesuit Sirmond and Cardinal Bona admit that the unleavened bread is an innovation.

IV. *Penitence.*—Is it not strange that, while the heretics of olden times did not object to this Sacrament, the Roman Confessional is abhorred by all the modern sects since the time of the Reformation? The Greeks, Armenians, Nestorians, Jacobites practise Confession, yet you hear of no complaints or scandals. The reason is: the Romans have developed their Confession into a system of Inquisition, into an espionage and direction of family affairs, into an engine of family quarrels, into a means of sowing scruples and perplexities by subtle and intricate cases of conscience, into a hiding-place where young and unmarried priests are exposed to the temptation of polluting their own minds and those of their penitents with the filth of unchastity. Voluminous historical evidences excuse us from quoting references. We are by no means disposed to make a sweeping charge and include every Roman priest in it. Thank God there are some (and we hope a good many) who are better than their system. But in one respect we are afraid we must include them all, viz., in the insidious way of weighing and measuring sin. Here the mischief begins—*and a truly diabolical mischief it is!*—by *creating a false conscience* and binding the people to it. If a man has been made to believe that a certain act is a mortal sin, it *is* a mortal sin, for man is judged by his conscience. Yet this conscience partly rests on Roman fictions! Can ever fiction take the place of truth? Can ever a false conscience be equivalent to a right one? St. Paul (1 Cor. iii. 13–15) answers this perplexing question: "Each man's work shall be made manifest; for the day shall disclose it, because it is revealed in fire; and the fire itself shall prove each man's work of what sort it is. If any man's work shall abide which he built thereon, he shall receive a reward. If any man's work shall be burned, *he shall suffer loss:* but he himself shall be saved; *yet so as through fire.*" This fatally tampering with the conscience of man was worked out into a system by the Spanish Dominican monk Bartholomew Medina (+ 1581), and was called *Probabilism,* because it laid down that a man in deciding a matter is not bound to follow the safer opinion (*tutiorism*), or even the more probable one (*probabiliorism*), but may acquiesce in the opinion of any man of authority (*probabilism*). The Jesuits soon got hold of this soul-destroying but inviting and lucrative system, toned it still more down, so as to make it perfectly serviceable for the use of a man of the world. Thus *laxity was sanctioned and codified.* Some propositions of the Jesuits, which were revoltingly bad, were, indeed, condemned by the Popes Alexander VII., Innocent XI., and Alexander VIII.—as a sop to pious Christians—but the root was not touched, and the tree was allowed to grow. At last Pope Gregory XVI. stretched out his hand and blessed this "tree of the knowledge of good and evil," by solemnly declaring that all confessors should be permitted to follow Alphonso Liguori, the arch-probabilist, and Pius IX. promoted Liguori to the exalted rank of "Doctor of the Church." Since the Jesuits almost monopolised Probabilism, within 150 years sixty-four Jesuits wrote books in defence of Probabilism. And from Emmanuel Sa to Matos (166 years), seventy-two advocated *Regicide* (king-murder). This line was rather compromising, and inconveniently disclosed the *revolutionary* character of the Romish Church. *Revolution* was the starting-point of Pope Zacharias. *Revolution* is by the present Papal Nuncio Meglia declared to be the only means of settling the European affairs satisfactorily. *Revolution by regicide* was the aim of Pope Pius V., now canonised as a Saint!! who planned the assassination of Queen Elizabeth of England.*

* In the correspondence of Philip II., published by Gachard (tom. ii. pp. 185-199), we read: "Pius V. writes to Philip II. that Ridolfi will come to speak with him (Philip) about an enterprise of high importance to God and the Christian nations, and entreats him to provide him with all the means necessary for the success of his plan, for this plan tended to the honour of God. Ridolfi was introduced to Philip II. to inform him of the Pope's commission, and the Secretary of the King gives the following report of it:—The matter in question is *to murder Queen Elizabeth.* The emissary exhibits the details of the plan. The plan is examined in a full Council of State. The Grand-Inquisitor, Archbishop of Seville, said it was necessary to support the conspiracy, and to declare that *they acted conformably to the Bulls of the Pope.* The Duke of Feria proposed to lay down as basis the just claims of the Queen of Scotland to the English throne. The Nuncio represented the enterprise as very easy. The King communicated the plan of the conspirators to the Duke of Alva. He entered into details, and said in his letters that *the object was to murder the Queen.* To serve God and the interests of the Church, *His Holiness offers his assistance*, and is

As the Roman Confessional in some breeds laxity, so in others it produces *scrupulosity*, arising from the casuistical niceties of the guides, and leading into such a maze of perplexities that not a few pious souls turned mad, or despaired and committed suicide.

We never read in any Roman Catechism that sins can be remitted *partly*. Yet when (twenty-eight years ago) we first entered the Church of SS. Pudens and Pudentiana (said to be the oldest church of Rome), we were startled at reading on the walls near the altar the following inscription: "Those who visit this church obtain on every day an indulgence of three thousand years and *the remission of the third part of their sins*" (*remissionem tertiæ partis peccatorum suorum*). For the whole inscription (in Latin and Italian) see our book "Catholic Orthodoxy" (London: Trübner, 1866), pp. 190-193. We do not doubt that even the most Ultramontane Roman will agree with us that this doctrine is *erroneous and heretical*. Yet it is published and tolerated under the eye of the infallible Pope! And Cardinal Manning says ("The Reunion of Christendom," p. 65): "We may be sure that whatsoever is prevalent in the Church, *under the eye of its public authority*, practised by the people, and not censured by its pastors, *is at least conformable to faith and innocent as to morals. Whosoever rises up to condemn such practices and opinions thereby convicts himself of the private spirit which is the root of heresy.*" We challenge Cardinal Manning to show that the *partly remission of sins* is a Catholic doctrine. HE CANNOT. Moreover, in the above passage he implicitly stamps *the infallible Pope Benedict XIV.* ("De Synodo

ready, though poor and ruined himself, *to deliver up for that purpose the chalices of the Church, yea, his own garments.*" When Castelar, in his great speech on religious toleration, read this documentary evidence in the Cortes, his opponent, Canon Manterola, *admitted the authenticity of the Pope's letter to Philip*, and clung to the poor consolation that in the letter the Pope did not ask the King to *find out* an assassin. But Castelar never asserted this. Why, after all, ask such a thing, if the assassin was perhaps already found out? We are no admirer of Queen Elizabeth, and less still of her religious principles; yet she might justly apply St. John xvi. 2 to the Pope: "The hour cometh that *whosoever killeth you shall think that he offereth service unto God.*" Is this not a dreadful state of a blunted and misled conscience? Here we see the practical fruit of Papal development! Yet Pius IX. commands the Romans to believe that *the Popes never transgressed the limits of their power*, consequently that such acts might be repeated at any time!

Diocesana," lib. xiii. cap. 18, no. 9, and the decree of the 18th September 1669 declaring indulgences of a thousand years and upwards *not genuine*) with the mark of *heresy!* How will the Cardinal disentangle himself from this network of contradictions? How can he clear himself from the charge of *heresy?* He who goes with Rome through thick and thin must be prepared to clash sometimes with inconsistent Rome, or to eat his own words quietly, submissively, blindly, but *unconvinced.*

A very serious innovation, rendering a great many Confessional absolutions extremely doubtful—an innovation for which we can only account by the increase of laxity invading the Roman Church since the great schism is the introduction of *Attrition* in Confession. This new-coined word, which the Orthodox Church does not know, means *imperfect contrition*, when man from fear or any worldly motive rejects sin, proposes not to do it any more, and (as the more pious authors add) has an *incipient* love. This Attrition is declared to be, by itself, insufficient for salvation, but *with Confession it is sufficient!* The Council of Trent (Sess. xiv. cap. 4) sanctioned it. The Roman Catholic Morinus (de Pœnit. lib. viii. cap. 2) states that the word Attrition, unknown to Holy Scriptures and to the Fathers, was introduced in the thirteenth century. And the celebrated theologian Liebermann (Institutiones Theologicæ, Moguntiæ, 1861, p. 621) adds: "The ancient opinion of the theologians was, that perfect contrition was absolutely necessary in order to receive the Sacrament effectually. It is a known fact that this opinion has, up to the Council of Trent, *prevailed* in the schools, and was even after that Council advocated by distinguished theologians. But now it is *obsolete* (!), and all teach in common that contrition with a perfect love is not required." Such is Roman *Perpetuity of faith!*

There is another grave error (the parent of another error that proved to be the last straw that broke the camel's back at the time of the Reformation) which disfigures the Roman doctrine of the Sacrament of Penitence. The Romans teach that by absolution the guilt and eternal punishment of sin (*culpa et pœna æterna*) are remitted, but that, as a rule, temporal punishments remain to be atoned for by works of satisfaction (penance). These temporal punishments are a *pœna vindicativa*, and not simply a *pœna medicinalis*. The Orthodox Church, on the contrary, teaches that absolution takes away the guilt and the punishment, both eternal and temporal, of sin, and no *reatus* (condition of a debtor) remains. It lies in the nature of the thing that the penitent has to make amends for what he has done wrong by injuring himself or others. But this is only a consequence of true contrition, not a punishment imposed by the priest. What our Church calls ἐπιτιμία (2 Cor. ii. 6) is by no means identical with the Roman "penance," but is simply a *medicinal* means, imposed on extraordinary occasions by the priest to assist the penitent in conquering bad habits. It is not a part of the Sacrament, not belonging to the priest as judge, but to the priest as physician.

This erroneous Roman doctrine naturally produced the Roman heresy of *Indulgences*, this cancer of faith and morals, so utterly unknown to the Orthodox Church, that Pope Gregory XIII., in his "*Professio Orthodoxæ fidei a Græcis facienda*" (Romæ, 1846, p. 12), is compelled to use the Latin word ἰνδουλγεντία. As we have in our Church no *pœnæ vindicativæ* left after absolution, there is no room for an institution for the purpose of remitting them. And as to remitting the *pœnæ medicinales*, it would be downright *immoral*. We have treated this subject at length in our book "*Der einzige sichere Ausweg für die liberalen Mitglieder der römisch-katholischen Kirche*" (Halle, 1870, p. 9 *seq.*), or in the French translation "*Unique moyen de sortir d'embarras pour les membres libéraux de l'église catholique romaine*" (Paris, 1872, p. 10 *seq.*) These Indulgences are, however, not only available for the living, but also *applicable to the dead*, though the "infallible" Pope Gelasius I. solemnly declared in the Roman Council (495): "We are requested to grant pardon also to the dead. But it is evident that *we cannot do this*, since it is said, 'Whatsoever you shall bind *on earth*.' He reserved those who are no longer *on earth*, *not to the human judgment*, *but to His judgment*. Moreover, *the Church dares not to arrogate what was not granted even to the blessed*

Apostles" (Mansi, tom. viii. p. 183 *seq.*) We know, indeed, that the Roman theologians teach that the Indulgences cannot with a certainty be applied to the dead, but only *per modum suffragii*, *i.e.*, leaving it to God's free will what He will do with them, and to what person He will apply them. But very few people know this restriction, and if they knew, their zeal in the matter would considerably cool down.

The Roman doctrine of Purgatory is closely connected with the doctrine of Indulgences. As we have fully treated the matter elsewhere ("*Der einzige sichere Ausweg*," p. 14 *seq.*, "*Unique moyen*," p. 15 *seq.*), we beg to refer to our exposition. Here we see what a havoc the Roman innovations have made in a single Sacrament, and how the simple truth has been fearfully adulterated.

V. *Holy Orders.*—This Sacrament has been so obscured by the Romans that they do not know for certain which is the matter (*materia*) of the Sacrament. Some think the only necessary and essential matter is the imposition of hands, while the delivery of the *instrumenta* is only accidental and integrant. Some consider the delivery of the instruments as the only essential matter, either confounding the imposition of hands with the delivery of the *instrumenta*, or believing the former to be merely an accidental and ceremonial act. The third opinion is that both acts are essential (Liebermann, l. c. tom. ii. p. 720). In this fix the Romans looked to the East, and, as they recognise the validity of the Orthodox orders, argued thus: "With the Greeks the imposition of hands is the only matter, consequently we must believe the same." To this must be added, "That the Ancient Church, the Latin included, for the first *ten centuries* has always ordained by the imposition of hands, without mentioning the delivery of the *instrumenta*" (Liebermann, *ibid.* p. 720).

That grave abuses prevailed in the Roman Church with regard to the age of the person to be ordained, we see already from the tenor of the 12th chap. Sess. xxiii. of the Council of Trent, in which it is forbidden to ordain *minors*. This order was issued in 1563. Yet in 1583 Joannes Jacobus Kelderer at Ratisbon was, as a baby, ordained a *deacon*, and died *when six days old.* The epitaph stating this fact is still preserved in the chapter-room of the Ratisbon Cathedral. That this case was not a solitary one show the Papal Constitutions, "*Cum ex sacrorum*" (Pius II. an. 1461), "*Sanctum*" (Sixtus V. an. 1589), "*Romanum*" (Clement VIII. an. 1595). However, as late as 1735 we find Don Louis of Bourbon made Cardinal-Archbishop of Toledo *when eight years old.* Duke Ernest, son of Albert IV. (the Wise), became (in the beginning of the sixteenth century) Coadjutor to Wigileus, Bishop of Passau, when he was *fifteen* years old. At the age of eighteen he succeeded the Bishop, threw thirty Anabaptists into the dungeon to disappear for ever, had Léonard Kaiser, a priest who had turned Lutheran, burnt alive, and twelve more Lutherans he delivered up to the flames. Still younger than Bishop Ernest was Leopold, Archduke of Austria, who, at the age of *ten*, became Coadjutor to the Bishop of Passau (1598), and at the age of *thirteen* was consecrated Bishop. When he came to the years of discretion he imitated Ernest, oppressed the Protestants, favoured the Jesuits, built a college for them, and founded the Pilgrim Church, Mariahilf. Then he renounced his Bishopric, unfrocked himself, and married a princess of Tuscany. The chronicles of many a Bishopric record similar scandals and abuses. And what shall we say of Pope Hadrian V., who was not even a priest when he died? (cf. Mansi, tom. xxiv. pp. 153-183). How could he, the Pope-*deacon*, claim to be the successor of the Apostle-*Bishop?* The Romans screen themselves behind the plea of jurisdiction; but if he was a *real* Pope, he must have been "*infallible.*" Now, unfortunately, the Deacons *never were by Christ or the Apostles intrusted with the office of teaching.* It matters little that the Pontificate of Hadrian lasted only one month and six days: it is the principle involved which we attack.

Sacrilegious reordinations took place in the Roman Church from the eighth to the twelfth century, on the heretic ground that simony or excommunication made ordinations *invalid*, and not only *irregular.* Reordination, Rebaptization, and Reconfirmation are unmeaning terms, for both the Roman and the Orthodox Churches teach that these Sacraments impress an *indelible character* (χαρακτῆρα ἀνεξάλειπτον —Synod. Hierosolym.) on the soul of the recipient. When, therefore, such an act takes place, it is only on the condition that a person is *not*, or (what is the same) *not properly*, baptized, or confirmed, or ordained, or that a doubt exists about it. In the first case, an unbaptized, &c., person receives Baptism, &c.; in the second case, only omniscient God knows whether the person was baptized, &c.; if the person was not baptized, &c., he receives Baptism, &c.; if he was baptized, &c., the act is *a mere ceremony, not imparting any sacramental grace.* However, such an act is not blameable, unless it rests on heretical principles (as in the Papal case before-mentioned), or is not supported by a real doubt.

Another fatal innovation is *the abuse of jurisdiction* for the purpose of curtailing the sacerdotal power imparted by the ordination. Only fancy! an absolution given a day after the episcopal license for hearing confessions has expired is considered not only irregular but *invalid*, whereas *in articulo mortis* it is valid at any time! Who has given power to the Church to *invalidate sacramental acts?* Peronne and Liebermann affirm, indeed, that the Roman doctrine on this point fully agrees with that of the Greek and of the whole Ancient Church, *without, however, producing a single proof for their assertion.* As jurisdiction concerns the law of *ecclesiastical* order, it could not be intended to paralyse the *divine* power of the Sacraments, since the lesser cannot overrule the greater. Though Confession to a priest supposes a *judicial* action on his part, the priest does act as a *judge instituted directly by Christ* through the Sacrament of Order, not as a *judge instituted by the Church.* Therefore a priest performing priestly functions without the permission of the Bishop of the diocese is censurable, and his ministrations are *irregular*, but by no means *invalid.* The Romans, confounding these two different and distinct judgeships and blending them into one, have prepared the road, or rather the inroad, of jurisdiction into the province of sacramental power. The sly and deep-laid plan is this: "If we can find a loophole to smuggle jurisdiction into the sacramental stronghold, the fortress is ours, and *Papal Supremacy, wielding this jurisdiction with absolute power, is also in possession of the Sacraments.*" Hence the arbitrary treatment of the Sacraments, as we have seen it hitherto. Hence the *casus reservati, i.e.*, those cases of conscience which the Pope and Bishops reserve to themselves to absolve from. The Orthodox Patriarchs and Bishops have never usurped such a power. The Romans, indeed, quote in support of their theory one solitary instance from antiquity, which a superficial reader may take as such, but which collapses on closer inspection, or rather changes into the contrary. It is this: Synesius, Metropolitan of Ptolomais in Cyrenaica, sends the case of Lampronianus, a priest convicted of a great crime, up to his Patriarch, Theophilus of Alexandria, for decision. Synesius was a great friend of Theophilus, who converted him, married him, and consecrated him Bishop when he was scarcely more than an inexperienced neophyte. What is more natural than that he should refer perplexing cases to his learned friend? Theophilus did *not claim it as his right*, nor did Synesius *divest himself of his right*, but expressly *authorised* Theophilus to decide in this case. The passage, to be found in the 66th Epistle of Synesius to Theophilus (2d edit. Petav. p. 215), runs as follows:—"I have sent up to the patriarchal chair the *power* to absolve (this criminal)." (*Τοῦ δὲ λῦσαι τὴν αὐθεντίαν εἰς τὴν ἱερατικὴν καθέδραν ἀνέπεμψα*). Now the reader may judge of the Latin translation of the Jesuit Peronne: "Solvendi (Lampronianum) porro *jus et auctoritatem* ad pontificiam sedem *rejeci.*" In this way harmless passages are pressed into the service of a settled theory.

The most cruel, most immoral, but (in a worldly sense) luckiest stroke of Papal policy was the introduction of "*Obligatory clerical celibacy.*" History has passed its verdict on the black deed. But a clever trick it was after all, by which the great "infallible" general obtained an army of soldiers totally free from all family ties, ready to march at a wink, ready to die, like the gladiators of old. *Cæsar morituri te salutant!* This was Gregory's idea, nothing else. The sanctimonious talk of converting the clergy into a host of angelic creatures was too naïve to be understood literally, as every one knows who has studied Gregory's times and human nature generally. Pure and genuine virginity is, indeed, the highest and noblest state of a Christian. But Christ intimates that "not all have room or capacity (χωροῦσι) for this word, *i.e.*, realise it, but (only those) to whom it has been given, *i.e.*, *who have the divine vocation*. He who *can* realise it, let him realise it." Those who have a vocation to married life will best serve God in that state. Celibacy is by no means identical with virginity, and in itself not preferable to a married life. But though Gregory knew the opinion of our Saviour, that the choice should be free and the divine vocation be consulted; though he knew the Canon of the Council of Gangra strictly condemning the opposition to married priests; though he knew the views of the Holy Fathers, he disregarded all and went his own way, tore asunder the *indissoluble* bond of legitimate marriages, demoralised the separated families, and sowed the seeds of hypocrisy and debauchery, growing rapidly into a plentiful crop. Had he never read St. Jerome describing the wicked state of the celibate clergy of his time? Had he not read St. Chrysostom? This holy man knew better the true spirit of Catholicity than Gregory VII., whose head was full of ambitious plans and suprematial aspirations. St. Chrysostom says (46 Hom. in Matt. xiii. 24): "The uppermost (virtue) is charity and clemency, and this is more than celibacy." And (63 Hom. in Matt.): "The Lord adds, 'He who can receive it, let him receive it,' . . . wishing, according to His ineffable kindness, *not to make the matter a binding law.*" And again (7 Hom. in Heb. v. 11–13): "If one cannot lead the same Christian life in wedlock as a monk (in celibacy), all is lost, and there remains only a small place for virtue. How should, then, still 'marriage be held in honour' (Heb. xiii. 4), *if it were such a great hindrance?*" The Ultramontane Dr. J. Zhishman ("*Das Eherecht der orientalischen Kirche*," Wien, 1864, p. 167) admits that the Orthodox Church always honoured *voluntary* celibacy, but never overvalued it. "In doing so she was far from considering the celibate life as a merit in the individual and, *without commanding or even implicitly counselling the one or the other*, kept a middle course between both directions." Hence the moral condition of the Orthodox clergy. Hence its popularity and patriotism. The Roman priest is a cosmopolitan, having no fatherland, no home, no hearth to defend. The Orthodox priest is in the first rank to defend his country and his altar, and shed his life's blood for them, as we saw still in our days. Forsooth! celibacy is not a heavy burden, if the celibate keeps a harem of fifty women, as Pope Alexander VI. did. It certainly was not a burden to Pope John XXIII. who, besides being guilty of rape and incest, *tercentas monachas stupravit, quas postea fecit abbatissas vel priorissas.* Schröckh in his "Church History," vol. xxxi. p. 378 *seq.*, may be consulted for further information. The hypocrite Pope Benedict XII. delivered a severe lecture to the immoral clergy of Narbonne, while he offered to Petrarca the cardinal's hat, "*dummodo soror ejus suo concederetur arbitrio*" (Hieron. Squarzafic. Vita Fr. Petrarch.) Pope Sixtus IV. established brothels in Rome, and drew a yearly income of 20,000 ducats from them. The Roman people styled him *leno vorax, pathicus, meretrix, delator, adulter*, &c. *Gaude, prisce Nero, superat te crimine Sixtus*, &c. See for the three distichs our "*Unique moyen*," p. 70, note. Agrippa (de Vanit. Scient. ep. 64) tells us how a bishop boasted that he had a yearly income of 11,000 dollars as taxes from the *Sacerdotes concubinarii.* Agrippa had travelled in Germany, France, England, and Italy, and published the book referred to in 1527. How desperate matters were looking in England we have shown in our paper "Obligatory Clerical Celibacy" (*Orth. Cath. Review*, vol. ii. pp. 244–256), and drawn a *documentary* picture which reminds us of the profligacy of heathen Rome at the time when Petronius, Martial, Juvenal, and Persius wrote. Archbishop Thomas of Arundel ("*eminentissima turris ecclesiæ Anglicanæ*"), his successor, Henry Chichele, founder of All Souls' College, Oxford, Hortig of Abingdon, Professor of Divinity at Oxford, Bishop Hallam of Salisbury, Richard Ullerston, Professor of Divinity at Oxford, give us desperate accounts of the clerical immorality of their time. Cf. Arthur Duck (*Vita Cichellii*, pp. 48–52),

Wharton (i. 122), Thomas Walsingham (*Hist. Angl.* p. 387 *seq.*), and Hardt in his celebrated work on the Council of Constance. The gentlemen and farmers of Carnarvonshire presented a complaint to King Henry VII. accusing the clergy of *systematic seduction of their wives and daughters.* No wonder that the whirlwind of the Reformation came and swept such a Church from the face of the land. Well might Photius say in his Encyclical (p. 50, ed. Montacut.): "They (the Roman Bishops and their clergy) produce many girls, who are wives without husbands, women suckling children, children who are not permitted to know their father; and such men deliver up to abomination those priests who *lead an exemplary life* (διαπρέποντας) *in lawful wedlock!*" In these straits pious Roman Bishops, as Durandus, Bishop of Mende in Languedoc, in 1296, turned their eyes towards the East, and wished to introduce the Eastern use, since it was the observance of Apostolic times.* But soon the Babylonian captivity at Avignon began, religion was swallowed up by politics and party strifes, and reforms were indefinitely postponed. The clerical life of this period was indescribably bad, so that Petrarch calls Avignon the "Babylon on the Rhone," and gives us a description in his sixteenth epistle (Basle edition of his works, 1581), which by far surpasses the worst descriptions of heathen vice. Only in hell the counterpart might be found. If any one is desirous of convincing himself of the truth of this assertion, let him consult Theiner's classical work on "Obligatory Clerical Celibacy" (Altenburg, 1828, vol. ii. pp. 619–621), where the Latin text is given in full.

And now let us for a moment return to London. On the 3d July 1881, Father Tylee preached in the evening a sermon (in the Roman Catholic Church in Rosoman Street), in presence of Dr. Weathers, Bishop of Amycla,

---

* "Cum pæne in omnibus conciliis et a plerisque Romanis pontificibus super cohibenda et punienda clericorum incontinentia, et eorum honestate servanda multa hactenus emanaverint constituta, *et nulla tenus ipsorum reformari quiverit correctio morum;* videtur pensandum, an expediret et posset provideri, *quod in ecclesia occidentali, quantum ad votum continentiæ, servaretur consuetudo ecclesiæ orientalis, quantum ad promovendos, potissime quum tempore Apostolorum consuetudo ecclesiæ orientalis servaretur.*"—Tractatus de modo celebrandi generalis concilii, pars. ii. rubr. 46, p. 166.

on the office of the Holy See, in which the following passage occurs: "Here is a royalty continuing for nineteen hundred years, and the most bitter enemies of the Church have only been able to find *two or three at most* of the sovereigns on whose character there *may* rest a stain." This is taken from the Ultramontane paper *The Universe*, July 9, 1881. Now, every tolerably well-instructed candidate of theology will be able to furnish the preacher at least with *a score* of Popes who were debauchees of the deepest dye.* In this way Roman Churchmen are taught historical *truth!* But if the Dominican M. J. H. Ollivier dares to clear even the character of Pope Alexander VI. ("*Le Pape Alexandre VI. et les Borgia*," Paris, 1870), we need not wonder if by and by the eleven Popes of the *πορνοκρατία*, the Avignon model Popes, and John XXIII. into the bargain, will be cleared and washed and whitewashed. The Roman Catholic A. Von Reumont, however, thinks that Ollivier's "*courage in falsifying facts*" is unbearable. Yet does this falsifying tendency in the Roman Church not show how deep the Jesuit principle that the end sanctifies the means has eaten into her flesh? If the Pope could, he would *remodel* history. This *per parenthesin.*

A Papal schism of forty years' standing ensued, followed by the stormy period of the Councils of Pisa, Constance, Basle, Ferrara, and Florence. But Pope Eugene IV., did he not stand out like a hero, great alike by his integrity and the other imposing qualities of his character? Such he is represented by Dr. Zhishman ("*Die Unionsverhandlungen zwischen der orient. und römischen Kirche*," Wien, 1858, p. 20 *seq.*) A greater misrepresentation can scarcely be found, for, looking behind the scenes, we find him to be an uncommonly mean character, of rough military habits, faithless, and a cruel murderer. Ffoulkes ("*The Church's Creed or the Crown's Creed?*" p. 22 *seq.*) has given us a truer picture. "Eugenius," says his most partial biographer—I am quoting from Giaconius —"was esteemed constant in adhering to his engagements,

* Génébrard, Archbishop of Aix (Chron. ad ann. 901), speaks of "*fifty* Popes so profligate that they deserve rather the name of apostates than that of apostolic men."

unless he happened to have promised anything which it were better to recall than to perform. . . . Blondus, the Pope's secretary, is lost in wonder at the vast sums of money expended by his master in *conciliating* the high dignitaries or indigent prelates of the Greek emperor with ***presents.*** Syropulus, one of the number, less scrupulously calls them ***bribes.*** . . . Cardinal Vitelleschi was suddenly seized and ***put to death,*** *without any trial, by his orders.*" Another murder Eugene committed by having the saintly Carmelite monk, Thomas Conecte, tortured by the Inquisition and ***burnt,*** *because he attacked the vices of the Roman Court.* The dark shadow of this crime persecuted him to his dying hour. Such was Eugene. And if we rub off the official gilding from the image of many a "good" Pope, what remains? Either a harmless insignificance, or cunning ambition disguised by the venerable cowl of a hermit. Kurtz, a very reliable Church historian, justly remarks: "Almost all the successors of Pius II. down to the Reformation were notorious for their lewdness and impiety, or at least thoroughly secular and profane." Bellarmine (Concio xxviii., Opp. tom. vi.) says: "Some years before the heresies of Luther and Calvin there was, according to the testimony of contemporary writers, neither justice in the ecclesiastical tribunals, nor discipline in the morals of the clergy, nor knowledge of sacred things, nor respect of holy things—in short, there was scarcely left any religion." The tide of moral corruption ran higher and higher, but could not be stemmed nor the flood be averted, since obligatory clerical celibacy, *as the mightiest supremacial tool,* was not to be sacrificed, not to be exchanged for the ancient practice of Apostolic tradition, as the East unchangeably kept it. The body of the Roman Church, rotten to the core, burst at last; but it was not the worst class of members that separated (as the Romans like to represent it). Oh, no; the *cloaca maxima* remained in Rome. The Protestants increased, and count now ninety millions. *A clear loss of ninety millions to the Roman Church!* Is this not again the finger of God writing on the wall the doom of schism? Ambition, imperiousness, and immorality arising from the obligatory clerical celibacy had brought Rome so low. Pope Hadrian VI. expresses himself thus in his instruction for the Nuncio Cheregati, whom he sent to the Diet of Nuremberg: "We know that for a long time abominable excesses have taken place at the Holy See, abuses in spiritual things, transgression of power; everything has been vitiated. The corruption has spread from the head to the members, from the Pope to the prelates; there is none who has done what is right, no not one" (Rainald, tom. xi. p. 363). The Council of Trent, a miserable patchwork, as far as Church reform is concerned,* altered little in the matter. The indirect influence of the Reformation effected more, so that in countries where the sharp eye

* Let the renowned Portuguese Archbishop of Braga, Bartholomeu dos Martyres, one of the most prominent members of the Council of Trent, state his opinion. Pallavicini has written about him in the 15th book, xi. 4, of his "*Istoria del Concilio di Trento.*" We quote from Fr. Luis de Sousa's "*Vida de D. Fr. Bartholomeu dos Martyres,*" livro ii. cap. 10: "He (Bartholomew) thought that, as the principal aim of this sacred and general congregation was to improve the world and to purify it from vices, it behoved to begin the work by its most important part, *i.e.*, the ecclesiastical, and by its most elevated part, *i.e.*, the prelates; and thence to pass to the less important things, and to everything in proportion as it requires remedying; and he said 'that they ought to proceed in an orderly way,' and all the more called [the proceeding] preposterous and disorderly: *but the votes he met with were against him*; that the reformation in [one's own] house, though undertaken with one's own hands, was not a palatable thing: and as it was an affair in which the higher and more weighty persons were most interested, *all dissembled* and went on laying hold of other matters, discussing and defining them, without touching the above matter. However, the Archbishop did not alter his mind, and, gathering strength from the very opposition, insisted, begged, persuaded, and gave advice in public and in private not to lose over things of little importance such a precious occasion for effecting great things: that they should begin presently by what is most proper, *i.e.*, to cleanse and purify the gold of the Church, *i.e.*, *the clergy, who was stained with corrupt manners of pleasure and pomp and with many vices springing therefrom.*"—"Lhe parecia que como o fim principal d'aquella sagrada e geral congregação era emendar a mundo, e purificalo de vicios, convinha começar a obra pela parte mais grave d'elle, que era o ecclesiastico, e pela melhor do ecclesiastico, que eram os prelados; e d'ahi passar as cousas de menos consideração, e a tudo o mais que havia que remediar; e isto dizia 'que era proceder com ordem,' e tudo o mais chamava prepostero e desconcertado: mas achava votos contra si; que reformação em casa, indaque seja tomada com as proprias mãos, não é cousa saborosa: e como negocio, em que os maiores e mais poderosos eram os mais interessados, dissimulavam todos, e iam pegando d'outras materias, discutindo, e definindo, sem tractarem d'esta. Porêm o arcebispo não mudou de animo; e tomando forças da mesma contrariedade, instava, rogava, persuadia, e aconselhava em publico e em particular, que não gastassem, em cousas de pouco importancia, uma tam preciosa occasião, como tinham entre mãos pera grandes effeitos: que começassem logo pelo que mais convinha, que era alimpar e apurar o ouro da igreja, que era o stado ecclesiastico, que stava escurecido com costumes depravados de delicias, e pompas, e com muitos vicios, que d'aqui brotavam." And a few pages farther on in the same chapter Sousa relates how "one [Father of the Council of Trent] after another *with one accord* (nemine discrepante) said with their usual courtesy 'that the most illustrious and most reverend cardinals *needed no reformation*'" (*cardeaes não haviam mister reformados*). The Portuguese scholar will have remarked that the spelling of Sousa is not the modern one.

of heretics exercises a wholesome control, the visible state of affairs is less objectionable than before. Scandals occasionally happening are hushed up. And as to the Popes of our age, let "a Winchester Incumbent" speak ("Historical Witness against the Church of Rome and its Counterfeit." London: James Nisbet): "Our own age has seen some of the worst [?] successors of the Apostle Peter. The scandalous life of Leo XII., his amours and numerous offspring by Madame Pfiffer of Lucerne, and again that of Gregory XVI., his levity and frivolous amusements, as minutely described in a recent work of a Roman Catholic writer, go to prove that the advancing civilisation and march of mind of the nineteenth century have had little or no effect in correcting the scandals of the pretended Vicars of Christ." If this statement is correct, it would bring us to the year 1846, to the Pontificate of the last Pope but one!

VI. *Matrimony.*—We have just heard how greatly Rome has damaged the Church by making clerical celibacy compulsory. If a man has a divine vocation for both the priesthood and married life, the Roman Church prevents him from following God's calling. How many lights of the Church were married priests, or sons of priests or bishops? Under Rome's new rule, we should have been deprived of them. We should not have had St. Gregory of Nazianzus, nor St. Gregory of Nyssa, who were sons of Bishop Gregory; nor St. Spyridion, Bishop of Trimython in Cyprus, who "was married and had children, yet was not on this account deficient in spiritual attainments" (Sozomen i. 11); nor St. Hilary, Bishop of Poitiers, who dearly loved his daughter Abra; nor Marcellus, Bishop of Apamea, and his brave sons (Sozomen vii. 15). Athanasius and Gregory of Nazianzus tell us that the number of married priests was very great, but they add no word of blame or reproach, but seem to lay a particular stress on the perfect freedom of choice.

The over-estimation of clerical celibacy, the identifying of celibacy and virginity, the exclusion of married men from the priesthood, naturally led to a depreciation of matrimony. The Manichean principle, "*matter is evil*," "*flesh is sin*" (not flesh (σὰρξ) as concupiscence, but as a physical component of man), lurked in the background, and they entirely forgot St. Chrysostom's word: "How could marriage be had in honour if it were such a hindrance?" Thus an Ultramontane writer ("*Du Mariage et du Célibat au double point de vue laïque et sacerdotal,*" Paris, 1863, p. 15) says: "For the Christians, marriage is less an end than a means: it is, in one sense, *the reduction of evil to its simplest expression*" (*la réduction du mal à sa plus simple expression*). Marriage is too low a state for a priest; this *sacrament* is only good enough for laymen. Yet how filthy the thoughts and words of those exalted celibates are concerning the *lawful marriage* of the Greek priests, we see from Cardinal Humbert's reply to Nicetas Pectoratus, sect. 34 (ap. Will: *Acta et scripta quæ de controversiis ecclesiæ Græcæ et Latinæ sæc. XI. composita extant,* Lipsiæ et Marpurgi, 1861, p. 150). He represents the married priests as "*recenti carnis voluptate toti resoluti et marcidi,*" going to the altar, saying Mass, handling the immaculate body of Christ, "*indeque sanctificatas manus ad tractandum membra muliebria mox referant.*" What a graphic description! not indeed of chaste marriage, but of *brothel-life,* as the Western celibate priests practised it, and had to pay taxes for it to their Popes and Bishops! And Cardinal Humbert shows himself to be strikingly acquainted with it. We wonder what Cardinal Manning, who is a widower, and therefore must know better, may think of the opinion of his brother-cardinal. If the Church has power to set up new matrimonial impediments, as time and circumstances may require, these impediments can only be such as make the marriage *irregular* (*impedimenta prohibentia*), and not such as *annul* it (*impedimenta dirimentia*). All the annulling impediments are of Apostolic origin, partly inherited from the Old Testament, partly introduced by Christ, and handed down by the Apostles to the Church. But what was at any time allowed in the Church never can be so far disallowed that it *annuls* marriage, though it might be made an *irregularity*. In short, the Church cannot *create* or *abolish* annulling impediments, but only *state* those existing from the times of the Apostles. Consequently the Orthodox Church declares the priest marrying after ordination to have incurred *irregularity*, but considers his marriage *valid*, and does not compel him to discontinue it. The Roman Church, on the contrary, unlawfully declares his marriage *invalid*, and excommunicates him if he continues it. This grave and vital difference involves the principle of an *unlimited power of the keys* vested in the Pope, which the Orthodox Church utterly repudiates as an *unwarrantable innovation*. This Papal power is believed to be so mighty that it can presume to *correct* or *improve away* the "very impedimentum dirimens" of adultery set up by Christ Himself. Before the Council of Trent, however, Cardinal Cajetan (Comment. in Matt. xix.) thought still differently, and so did the Penitential books. These books (manuals for the use of Confessors, containing canons and resolutions) originated in the East, and were adopted by Theodore, Archbishop of Canterbury, a Greek monk and native of Tarsus in Cilicia, but degenerated by and by, and were disused in the twelfth century. Walter (Kirchenrecht, 13th edit. p. 196, note 7) is of opinion that Theodore never wrote a book, but Hildebrand says that the authentic text of Theodore's book was published for the first time in 1840 by the Record Office in the "Ancient Laws and Institutes of England." Of the Greek Penitential Canons, those of Patriarch Nicephorus (Dom. Pitra. Spicileg. Solesm. iv. 381–415) and of John the Faster are best known. A copious collection of Greek Penitential Canons is to be found in Codex Bodleian, 264 fol. 160 *seq.*

We saw the rigorous mien of Rome as defender of the indissolubility of matrimony, finding fault even with Christ on the subject of adultery; but though the Romans shut, with a great noise, the front-door, they opened the back-door and numerous commodious outlets for the convenience of the nupturient public. If they have only their pocket full of money, the *Dataria Apostolica* (founded in the thirteenth century) can easily find means and ways how to gratify their wishes. Even if the married couples are tired of each other, and wish to change hands, they need not despair; there is balm for them in Gilead. Great * and petty

* When Napoleon I. returned home in 1809, in the full glory of victories, Fouché told him: "*Il faut que Votre Majesté se résolve à un acte indispensable, il lui faut un divorce et un nouveau mariage.*" Napoleon, however, was ecclesiastically married to Josephine in 1804, on the eve of his coronation. Pope Pius VI. recognised his marriage, or he could not have anointed him. Yet in 1810, when Napoleon was going to marry Maria Louise, the priests found suddenly out that

sovereigns know this. Whatever else Rome may be, we cannot help commending her because she has done wisely; she called the Lord's debtors, and said to each of them: "Take thy bond, and sit down quickly and write a hundred scudi, or a thousand (as the case may be); and as thou hast wished, so be it done unto thee." Indeed the sons of Rome are in their generation wiser than the sons of Orthodoxy. The latter are still clinging to the old warning: "Get you no gold, nor silver, nor brass in your purses" (St. Matt. x. 9). The former think it more practical to borrow the full purse from Judas. Rome has certainly carried on a thriving business since it introduced the traffic of *Dispensations* in matrimonial matters. No man of business surpasses Rome in talent of organisation and in improving his resources. THE ORTHODOX CHURCH DOES NOT KNOW THE INSTITUTE OF DISPENSATIONS, and has not even a name for it; for the modern word, *συγκατάβασις*, is not an ecclesiastical term. Now let us hear what the zealous Ultramontane Dr. J. Zhishman ("*Das Eherecht der orientalischen Kirche,*" Vienna, 1864, p. 713) remarks on this point: "The Patriarchates have never usurped the power of admitting an exception from any ecclesiastical law which has been recognised from times immemorial, and *proofs are entirely wanting* for their having pleaded the principle of condescension or *οἰκονομία* for this purpose. . . . If the dispensations had ever been customary in the Church, the Patriarchal Synods would not have so determinately opposed those interpretations which tried to derive from single canonical documents the possibility of an exception." * One cannot help reading between the lines the suppressed admiration of the author for the Orthodox practice, as opposed to the abuse of Roman dispensation.

---

the parish-priest had not been present at the former marriage, and that it therefore had been null. And in the six preceding years no doubt or misgiving about the validity of the former marriage occurred to anybody, not even to the parish-priest, who knew all about it!!!

* "*Es haben sich die Patriarchate niemals die Macht angeeignet, von irgend einem seit den ältesten Zeiten anerkannten Kirchengesetze eine Ausnahme zuzulassen, und es fehlt durchaus an Zeugnissen, dass sie das Princip der Nachgiebigkeit oder der sogenannten Oekonomie dafür geltend gemacht hätten. . . . Wäre die Dispensation in der Kirche jemals üblich gewesen, so hätten die Patriarchal-Synoden nicht mit einer solchen Entschiedenheit jene Interpretationen bekämpft, welche aus einzelnen kanonischen Documenten die Möglichkeit einer Ausnahme abzuleiten suchten.*"

The scandals of the Roman Church severing matrimonial bonds, after many years' standing, for "want of consent" (*ex defectu consensus*), and in spite of children having been born in this union, are not so unfrequent, though the Roman Catholic canonist Walter (*Eherecht*, p. 656) shows that the fact of cohabitation is considered to be a "tacit consent." Still more frequently "mixed marriages" are annulled if the parties happen to be in a country where the Council of Trent has been officially published. The same is the case with marriages of heretics if one party turns Roman Catholic. The difference of religion (*disparitas cultus*) is a prolific source of divorce. How many marriages solemnised in the Roman Church would have been considered in the ancient Church (and are considered in the Orthodox Church) *adulterous*, *incestuous*, or mere *concubinages!*

VII. *Unction of the Sick.*—The Protestants unanimously reject this Sacrament, though St. James v. 14, 15, contains all the requisites of a true Sacrament. "But was it then instituted by Christ?" Of course it was. How could otherwise St. James have presumed to connect the *forgiveness of sin* (a *divine* privilege, St. Matt. ix. 2–6) with the *Prayer-Oil?* (εὐχέλαιον, as our Orthodox Church expressively calls this Sacrament). The Apostles nowhere call themselves *Institutors*, but only *Stewards* (or *Dispensers*, οἰκονόμους) of the mysteries (Sacraments) of God (1 Cor. iv. 1). "But where do we read in the Bible that Christ instituted this Sacrament?" We read in Acts iii. 1 that Christ, during the forty days between His resurrection and ascension, instructed His Apostles, "speaking of the things pertaining to the kingdom of God." These private lessons, of which the Bible offers no details, were the subject of the Apostolic teaching, as it was deposited in the Churches they founded, and faithfully transmitted to posterity. The use of this Sacrament in the Church was already hinted at by Origen (end of the second century) *in Lev. Hom.* ii. 4; St. Chrysostom (*de Sacerd.* iii. 6); St. Cyril of Alexandria (*De Adorat. in spir. et vert.* lib. vi. tom. i. p. 211, Paris, 1638); Victor, a priest of Antioch, in the beginning of the fifth century (*Comment. in Marc.* vi. 13, tom. i. p. 103, edit. C. F. Matth., Rigæ, 1775); and Cæsarius of Arles, fifth century, *Serm.* 265, 3 (in the Appendix to tom. v. of St. Augustine's works, Antwerp, 1700), speak still more clearly of our Sacrament. Pope Innocent I. at last, in his correspondence with Decentius, Bishop of Eugubium, in 416, speaks most explicitly of this Sacrament. That it was then an ancient Apostolic custom we see clearly from the retention of this Sacrament by the heretics who separated from the Church in the fifth century.

The theological manuals generally copy one from another the phrase: "So believe unanimously the Latin, Greek, Armenian, Nestorian, and Monophysite Churches." This is however only true in a qualified sense. The word *μυστήριον*, as well as the Latin *Sacramentum*, the Syriac *Roso*, and the Armenian *Khorkurt*, had originally the general meaning, "a holy thing, a holy performance." In this sense there were a great many "Sacraments;" in fact, an indistinct number of Sacraments. And "Mysteries" there were still more, *e.g.*, *μυστήριον τῆς ἀνομίας* (the mystery of iniquity, 2 Thess. ii. 7). In this general meaning, the oath, the washing of feet, the burial of the dead, the taking of the veil, &c., were called Sacraments. But among these sacred acts there were *seven* of an *essentially* different kind. If all the other so-called Sacraments impart grace in consequence of the pious disposition of the performer (*ex opere operantis*), and are empty ceremonies if such a disposition is wanting, these seven do not derive their efficacy from the disposition of the recipient (though the unworthy state of the recipient might frustrate the grace offered by God in the Sacrament), but if the proper minister employs the proper form and matter, the effect is *sure* and infallible, *i.e.*, they act (as the Romans express it) *ex opere operato.* In course of time the loose and general expression of "Sacrament" was dropped, and the name exclusively appropriated to the seven. This *septenary number* is professed by Latins, Greeks, Armenians, Nestorians, and Monophysites. There is no difference in the real character of these Sacraments, as far as they act *ex opere operato.* It is a dogmatical error of the Anglicans to suppose that there are only *two properly so-called Sacraments*, and that the five others are ordinances or rites *improperly called Sacraments*, a sort of *secondary* Sacraments, *i.e.*, no Sacraments at all. Moreover the Anglicans contradict themselves by calling Baptism and Eucharist the two only Sacraments "generally *necessary* to salvation." If they believe this (as in practice they do *not*), how could they have approved of and adopted the abolition of "children's communion"? But in this, as in many other points, we find that the Reformers stuck more faithfully to the *errors* than to the *truths* of their Roman mother.

We remarked before that the "Unction of the sick" is recognised by the Nestorians and the Monophysites only in a qualified sense. With the Nestorians it has nearly dwindled away, and nothing is left but "the sign of the vivifying cross" (*rushma da tsiliba machyona*). What they call "the oil of anointing" (*meshcha d'mashichutha*) is not this Sacrament, but Chrism or Confirmation administered with Baptism in one act. And the Armenians reckon indeed the "anointing the sick" among the Seven Sacraments, but administer it only to the priests. With the sick laymen only the prayers are said, but no anointing takes place, as the anointing is not deemed essential. Yet Chosrov says: "Prayer gives efficacy to the oil, and *completes* the remedy given for healing the sickness." Thus we have two instances, how schism leads to tampering with the ancient doctrine of the Church. A third instance is the Roman Church, which altered the Prayer-Oil into *Extreme Unction*. This change took place after the great schism in the twelfth or thirteenth century (Mabillon, *Præf. in sæc. I. Benedict*, n. 98; cf. Macaire, *Theologie dogmatique orthodoxe*, tom. ii. p. 552). In this way the Romans defeat one object of the Sacrament ("and the prayer of faith shall save the sick, and the Lord *shall raise him up*"). With the Romans this Sacrament is the much-dreaded companion of the Viaticum and the almost sure forerunner of death, often administered when the person is already insensible. With the Orthodox this Sacrament is what it was in the Ancient Church. When a person is *really ill* (not only slightly indisposed), he may *at any time* ask for this Sacrament, and is bidden *not to wait* till the fatal crisis sets in. Dr. Myriantheus is perfectly right in contradicting W. Palmer, "Dissertations on the Orthodox

Communion," p. 130 *seq.*; cf. W. Crouch, "*The Sacrament of Extreme Unction,*" p. 44 *seq.* The late Archpriest Eugene Popoff told us that in Russia the sick people soon resort to this Sacrament, and that *a great many wonderful instances of healing occur.* Indeed, God's arm is not shortened!

Another Roman innovation in administering this Sacrament is that only one priest dispenses it, while the Orthodox Church, with the Apostle St. James, employs several, if they can be had. In the Roman Church it is even *strictly forbidden* (as Pope Benedict XIV. remarks) that more than one priest administer this Sacrament, though other *non-officiating* priests may be present (Perrone, *Prælect. theolog.* tom. ii., Paris, 1842, p. 428, note 3). The benediction of the oil used in this Sacrament was, from times immemorial, performed by the officiating priests, but Rome reserved it to the Bishops. No wonder Rome, in more and more centralising the priestly power, followed only the centripetal force of Papacy.

Now let the reader judge himself whether the Roman Church is entitled to claim *Perpetuity of Faith.* It would certainly be easy enough to write an "*Histoire des Variations de l'Eglise romaine.*" Not only the fundamental Church constitution was subverted by the Popes, new dogmas introduced, Holy Canons set at nought, or even reversed; none of the Seven Sacraments was spared, but every one was defiled by the grossest abuses and unwarrantable innovations. AND ALL THIS CHANGE TOOK PLACE AFTER THE GREAT SCHISM, WHEN THE HOLY SPIRIT HAD LEFT THE APOSTATE ROMAN CHURCH, AND THE HUMAN SPIRIT REPLACED HIM. Our Saviour says: "By their fruits ye shall know them." We have inspected, in these pages, many of the fruits of the Papal tree, and found them rotten and pestiferous. But the visible fruits can naturally only be an occasional eruption of what is going on within the system. The same principles are still at work inside the Roman body as in the worst times of Papacy; and if the phenomena are less revolting now, it is the spirit of the age that no longer permits the wild outbursts of fanaticism, as we might have witnessed them in South America a couple of years ago. It is simply the "*iniquitas temporum*" which prevents Rome from re-kindling the stakes in Smithfield. The Romans, and a good many Romanising Anglicans, will, no doubt, ridicule these words. Yet the greatest and most learned champion of Papacy in our days, Cardinal Hergenröther, says: "The Church does *not, in principle, renounce any rights which she once has exercised*" (*Katholische Kirche und christlicher Staat*, Freiburg, i/B 1872, p. 804, note 1). We hope that those bloody times will never come back again, but the Romans have no reason to lay the blame on the time, and not on the Church. Was the character of the time not a product of the Church's education? Had the Protestants not learned the practice of burning heretics from their Roman *mother*, as they had learned many other bad things from her? The Roman Church in England is now meek as a lamb. History knows times when she could bite and devour with the teeth of a wolf. But whether lamb or wolf, she is always *still the same, and her principles have not altered.* The lamb is growing fast, and the Jesuit weeds are spreading marvellously and overgrowing England, stifling all healthy fruit. But in spite of all this, you hear not a few Anglicans speaking, with a morbid affection, of their "dearly beloved old Roman *mother*," forgetting all the while that this unnatural mother was *divorced* from her heavenly husband, Jesus Christ, the Head of the Catholic Church, and, as a *schismatic* outlaw, feeds on the husks of worldly dominion and spiritual tyranny. And this Roman outcast dares to call the Orthodox Church *schismatic*, because she did not choose to leave her father's home and follow her sister into a far country, and waste with the same her substance with riotous living. Therefore her fast Roman sister calls her all sorts of names: *crystallised, fossilised, mummified, petrified*, and (the very reverse of the former epithets) *schismatic!* We have seen some fruits of the *Roman schism;* but what is the Orthodox "schism"? Philaret, late Metropolitan of Moscow, will tell it us. In his "*Entretiens d'un sceptique et d'un croyant sur l'Orthodoxie de l'Eglise orientale*," Paris, 1862, p. 48, he says: "It is now a thousand years that she (the Eastern Church) exists since the separation from the Western Church; and during this time she has been preserved intact in the South and the East, in spite of the longest and hardest persecutions; and in the North she becomes great and strong, and flourishes more and more. *A schism has—as history proves it—never known such a protection by Providence*" (*un schisme, ainsi que l'histoire le démontre, n'a jamais connu une telle protection de la Providence*). The Orthodox always knew to appreciate their Church as the only true Catholic Church, and did not allow themselves to be decoyed into the Roman fold, in spite of all the trouble which Rome took to seduce or compel them.* How glad were the million and a half of United Greeks (Russians) of Lithuania, once forced by Polish tyranny into the Roman Communion, when Joseph Siemashko brought them back to their old Orthodox Church! And how loose is the bond with Rome of the Sicilian United Greeks, and how strong their inclination towards Constantinople! We heard it in Sicily from the mouth of the Greeks themselves. In Athens we heard that no Greeks join the Roman Church, and that it was quite a mistake to transfer the Roman Episcopal See from Syra to Athens. The Greek will absolutely not listen to Rome's voice. The clever and intriguing Jesuits at Constantinople know this from experience. If they catch a fish, it is sure to be unsound, and its loss is only a gain for the Orthodox Church. Such a fish was

* Let the bitterest enemy and persecutor of the Orthodox Church, Sigismund, king of Poland, confirm our words. In the instruction for his envoy to Pope Julius III. he says: "We know also from daily experience *how pertinaciously these people cling to their rites, how difficultly they are torn from the same, how inconstant their remaining in the true religion of the Roman Church is.* . . . As they, however, before obtaining a dignity, must submit to the doctrine and authority of the Roman Church, *very seldom one is found who does not prefer to live as the most despised man, provided he is allowed to retain his rites, rather than to obtain the highest place of honour and dignity by joining the Roman Church.*" "Nos quoque ipsi . . . . quotidie animadvertimus, quam pertinax sit ea gens in suis ritibus amplectendis, quam difficulter ab eis avellatur, quam inconstanter in vera Romanæ Ecclesiæ religione persistat. . . . Quia tamen ante adeptam dignitatem submittere se Romanæ Ecclesiæ doctrinæ atque auctoritati illos necesse est, rarissimus est, qui non malit contemptissimus vivere, dummodo illi suos ritus retinere liceat, quam in excelsissimo quoque honoris ac dignitatis gradu ad Romanam se Ecclesiam adjungens collocari."—Joseph Fiedler: "*Ein Versuch der Vereinigung der Russischen mit der Römischen Kirche im xvi. Jahrhundert,*" Wien, 1862, p. 86. The copy of the document is taken from the royal-imperial house-archives. Fiedler is a staunch Roman Catholic of the correct Ultramontane type.

Pitzipios. They squeezed the orange out and then threw it away. The poor man had a sad end.

We saw how the Orthodox Church was by God's wonderful Providence kept intact as a faithful guardian of Christ's doctrine; but history conveys another lesson to us respecting Rome. When she left her Father's home, she first ran on lustily in search of honour, power, and wealth. She obtained what she sought, and got a worldly sceptre into the bargain, a sceptre that swayed empires and kingdoms. Gregory VII. defied the mightiest king, but Innocent III. was still mightier than Gregory, though not so mighty as to force the East into a union with the West. Innocent might dethrone Otto IV., Emperor of Germany, and John, King of England, might enthrone Frederic II., might give a king to Bulgaria and Wallachia, might return his kingdom to John as a Papal fief, might bless the Latin Empire at Constantinople; but the Orthodox, though bodily trampled down and trodden upon, were *the only power* Innocent could not prevail upon. Under Innocent, Papacy reached the zenith of its worldly glory, the human omnipotence promised by the Prince of this world. This glory lasted a hundred years, till Boniface VIII. saw the beginning of the end. Boniface, an insatiably ambitious and most energetic but utterly worldly man, overstrained his power, issued the unparalleled Bull "*Unam sanctam*" (which all Infallibilists recognise as an *ex cathedra* document), engaged in conflicts with princes, and found his authority so far gone that Philip of France could address him "Your Foolishness" (*tua fatuitas*), and William of Nogaret could take him prisoner. Yet he added the second crown to the tiara. (Urban V. superadded the third at a time when Papacy had already sunk considerably.) Dante* (*Inferno*, canto xxvii.) places Boniface, as simonist, in hell

* Dante was not only a poet and politician, but also a learned and trustworthy theologian. "Dantes theologus, nullius dogmatis expers." This line is the first of his epitaph by Giovanni del Virgilio. The "Divina Commedia" was studied and commented upon by Visconti, Archbishop of Milan, John, Bishop of Serravalle, and a host of the most prominent theologians. One of the first French translators of this work, Abbé Grangier, says in his dedication to Henry IV.: "En ce noble poëme, il se découvre un poëte excellent, un philosophe profond, et un *théologien judicieux*."

between the Popes Nicholas III. and Clement V., and puts in his mouth these words: "My works were not those of a lion, but of a fox. The tricks and covered ways I knew all, and I managed them so artfully, that the fame of them went forth to the end of the world."

> ". . . L'opere mie
> Non furon leonine, ma di volpe.
> Gli accorgimenti, e le coperte vie
> Jo seppi tutte, e sì menai lor arte,
> Ch'al fine della terra il suono uscie."

The Roman people coined this sentence on him: "He crept in as a fox, ruled as a lion, and died as a dog."

Papacy, so brilliant and imposing to look at for a hundred years, soon showed that "not all is gold that glitters," for it suddenly took a plunge and disappeared in the muddy waters of Avignon. The seventy years of Babylonian captivity disclosed a state of rottenness in the Papal Church which the Roman historians are grieved to admit. But a still more scandalous state of things followed, known as the "*Papal Schism*" (1378–1409). There were two or three Popes at a time, fighting and excommunicating each other to their heart's content. No Roman knew where was the oracle of his Church. At last things got to such a pass that the so-called "reformatory Councils" of Pisa, Constance, and Basle had to cut the Gordian knot, applying the principle of superiority, CONDEMNED AS HERETICAL BY THE PRESENT PAPACY AND THE VATICAN COUNCIL!! Yet the present Pope is only a successor of Martin V., who acquiesced in the Council of Constance deposing the three simultaneous Popes, and consented to be elected instead of them. Now, if the Council transgressed its power (as the present Romans *must* believe it did), Martin was an *illegitimate* Pope, and the Church had lost its head.

The moral state of Western Christendom was shocking. No pen can describe it. In fact, the Roman Church, the vaunted "abode of the Holy Ghost," was a *Pandemonium*. The Italian clergy, tired of *natural* vices, practised *Sodomy* (exempt from taxation). "At the [*reformatory!*] Councils of Constance and Basle thousands of *prostitutes* from all countries flocked together for the use of the pious Fathers [who were to frame the Canons for the improvement of morals!]" (Kurtz, *Lehrbuch der Kirchengeschichte*, 7th edit. Mitau, 1874, vol. i. p. 382). But our Saviour says: "A good tree *cannot* bring forth evil fruit, neither can a corrupt tree bring forth good fruit. Every tree that bringeth not forth good fruit is hewn down, and cast into the fire. Wherefore by their fruits ye shall know them."

The hewing down of the Roman tree began at the Reformation. We have shown before how Rome sustained a clear loss of ninety million souls in consequence of the Reformation. To retrieve the loss the wiles of Jesuitism were established and organised (1540), heretics were burnt, and a thirty years' war was kindled, so cruel and devastating that history scarcely knows where to find its like. The Romans did not retrieve their loss, but, on the contrary, the war ended with a peace which established the legal basis of the Protestant Church, and therefore was never recognised by the Popes. *But nobody cared for the Pope's approbation*—so deep Rome's power had sunk already; all monarchs, both Roman and Protestant, recognised the stipulations of the Peace of Westphalia, and Rome was compelled to *submit to a hard fact*, *i.e.*, to reckon with the results of the Peace of Westphalia as with a given factor. Rome was allowed the luxury of protesting. It was allowed to stultify itself to any degree, for its power was gone.

The Romans had already for some time felt that in the West their sun was setting, and as they particularly look out for numbers, Pope Gregory XV. turned his eyes towards the far East, and founded (1622) the grandest missionary institution the world had ever seen, the *Congregatio de Propaganda Fide*. The Roman Church was always a *proselytising* body. This would certainly not be a blame, but a high praise, if the Roman Church were the true Catholic Church; for IT IS THE BOUNDEN DUTY OF HIM WHO POSSESSES THE TRUTH TO SPREAD IT. But the *missionary spirit* is in itself not a mark of the true Church; for did not the Nestorians of old extend their doctrine as far as India and China? And the Wesleyans, Baptists, and Mormons are proselytising on a grand scale. So were the Pharisees: "Woe unto you, scribes and Pharisees, hypocrites! for ye compass sea and land to make one proselyte, and *when he is made, ye make him twofold more the child of hell than yourselves*" (St. Matt. xxiii. 15). So it is with many of the Roman proselytes. They are allured into the Roman Church before their conviction is settled. Go and ask the numerous Anglicans who after a while leave the Roman Church. So it was with the first expedition of the Propaganda, viz., the Jesuit mission of Adam Schall to China (1628). Many thousands of Chinese were converted, but the Dominicans soon found out that they were still essentially heathens. And when the Pope sent Thomas of Tournon to investigate the matter, the Jesuits had him imprisoned in Macao, and the Papal Legate died in prison! So the Jesuit political ascendancy was saved and the Pope was made a fool of, though the fourth vow of the Jesuits is "unconditional obedience to the Pope"! Never mind; the ground lost in Europe was to be recovered in China, so much the more as Francis of Xavier's work in Japan was totally destroyed about this time.

In Europe the Papal influence waned more and more. The French Encyclopedists uprooted Christianity and produced the French Revolution. Catholic France lost its faith —why? Because it had been an outward cloak of an empty soul. France now showed the fruits of her Church's education. Could Voltaire (himself a pupil of the Jesuits) have conquered the French if the Church had conscientiously done her work? Napoleon restored the Church, and the first present of Pius VII. was the resuscitation of the Society of Jesus. The work of the Jesuits was for a long time underground. Their polished manners and aristocratic associations had their effect. People forgot the history of the past and enjoyed the company of the present. The storm of 1848 cleared the air for the pleasant, modest, and zealous Fathers, and in a short time Jesuit churches, colleges, and institutions sprang up everywhere through the length and breadth of Europe. Rome seemed to revive; its principles were preached, hailed, and followed. But in the meanwhile Garibaldi rose, a man without religion, but a fervent patriot

—and all the people ran after him, helped him to drive the Bourbons away, and showed an utter dislike of the Jesuits, whom they knew better than their Northern brethren. The Pope lost his possessions by inches, and his subjects, *though* (or perhaps *because*) trained in the Papal school for centuries, welcomed the victor. Now the Pope is a Prisoner in the Vatican, supported by the Peter's Pence of the Faithful —a respectable source of income, considering Cardinal Antonelli's millions. Meanwhile the seed of the Jesuit training has developed into the *poisonous and revolutionary* plant known under the name of *Kulturkampf*, *i.e.*, enacting Papal Supremacy at the expense of monarchical power. Thus, for the sake of power, the Pope sacrifices Bishops and priests, and leaves thousands of Roman Catholic laymen without Mass and Sacraments. Such is the spirit of Papacy. "*By their fruits ye shall know them.*"

Before we wind up this chapter on the Roman Church, we have still to answer three questions:—

1. How is it that the Roman Church, which holds the same principle as the Orthodox Church, viz., that *no new dogmas can be made, but only those contained in the Apostolic Deposit of Faith can be proclaimed or defined*, has nevertheless made new dogmas? The Romans naturally deny that these dogmas are new, and maintain that they are but a *development** of

* The word *development* is the charm of all modern Theology, and the mainstay of Romanism, Unitarianism, Broad-Churchism, and Rationalism generally. Mr. Nevins says: "As with the development and growth of body and mind in the creature man, so in the Christian Church *there must be growth or there will be death.*" In this sentence there is truth and untruth mixed together. Let us consider the *individual* member of the Church. He certainly must grow in the faith, or he will die. However, this growth is not a bodily but a spiritual growth; it is not *extensive* but *intensive*. This necessary growth and development of faith is masterly expressed by St. Paul (Eph. iii. 14–19): "For this cause I bow my knees unto the Father, from whom every family in heaven and on earth is named, that He would grant you, according to the riches of His glory, that ye may be strengthened with power through His Spirit in the *inward* man; that Christ may dwell in your hearts through faith; to the end that ye, being rooted and grounded in love, may be strong to apprehend with all the saints *what is the breadth, and length, and height, and depth*, and to know the love of Christ, which passeth knowledge, that ye may be filled unto all the fulness of God." By this inward growth of faith "we attain . . . unto a full-grown man, unto the measure of the stature of the fulness of Christ: that we may be no longer children, tossed to and fro and *carried about with every wind of doctrine, by the sleight of men, in craftiness, after the wiles of error;* but, speaking truth in love, may *grow up* in all things unto Him which is the Head, even Christ; from whom all the body fitly framed and knit together through that which every joint supplieth, according to the working

Apostolic truth, and that the Church possesses the right of developing doctrines. The Orthodox Church rejects the principle of doctrinal development, and denies that the Church ever possessed such a right. When a heresy arose, the Church simply *stated* the respective doctrine as deposited and taught in the various Apostolic Churches. If Willis Probyn Nevins ("*Development versus Fossilised Christianity*," London : Pickering, 1881, p. 30) says : "The Greek Church developed as rapidly as the Roman till the schism," we deny it. The Orthodox Church *stated* the doctrine disputed on the ground of the *de facto* deposit in the single Churches, not as an umpire in any theological questions whether they form part of the Apostolic deposit of faith or not. Hence the difference between the Seven Œcumenical Councils and the later General Councils of the West. An Eastern who denied the divinity of Christ, before the Council of Nicæa had fixed it dogmatically, would have been considered as much a heretic

---

in due measure of each several part, *maketh the increase of the body unto the building up of itself in love*" (Eph. iv. 13–16). This is what we Orthodox understand by the growth and lawful development of faith—a development extending through the life of the individual, and of the Church at large, into eternity. Is this *no life?* Is such a life *fossilisation?* Mr. Nevins's Church-life consists in *ever-increasing bulk*, in an *aggregation or agglutination of a continuous mass of dogmas*. Our Church-life is an *organic process* going on within the individual and within the Church at large, according to the injunction of St. Paul. We do not, and never did, want any new dogmas. Our Seven Œcumenic Councils were simply caused by heresies attacking our Apostolic trust, and did nothing else but oppose the old faith to the new inventions. In this way the old faith had to be secured by new words : *τριὰς, ὁμοούσιος, θεοτόκος*, &c., against the wiles of the heretics who abused the simple expressions of the Apostolic teaching. But though the word was new, the thing signified was as old as the Apostles. And when the Reformation brought new heresies to light, our Church was not slow in stating her belief in the *μετουσίωσις, presushchestvlenie* (Transubstantiation), a sign that her dogmatic life did not end with the great schism.

All things suffer change save God the Truth ; therefore our Church's belief remains unchangeably the same, because it is *the revelation of God the Truth*. The organs of the Church are, indeed, human channels, and as such *naturally* fallible, but when they co-operate in expressing the Voice of the Church, they are *supernaturally* infallible, according to Christ's promise. Of course all those who deny the supernatural guidance of the Church (which Mr. Nevins, however, does not deny), and simply stick to the natural growth and development of a merely human and historical institution, must here part with us. They are at liberty to disagree ; but to declare a Church *fossilised* because, from their point of view, they cannot observe the beating of its pulse, the circulation of its blood, and the movement of its inward organic life, is certainly not wise. There are things beyond the limited horizon of the natural man, of which he has no perception, which, however, to deny would be presumptuous. When we were young the Roman Church had the same view of the matter as we, together with the Orthodox Church, have now ; but what is the Roman belief at present ?

before the Council as after it; whereas a Roman Catholic could up to 1870 deny Papal Infallibility and still be a good Catholic. Moreover, in none of the Seven Œcumenical Councils was a doctrine mooted and set aside as *not yet ripe for decision*, as was the case in the Council of Trent concerning the dogmas of the Immaculate Conception and the Infallibility of the Pope. Such instances of *growing into a dogma* are not to be found in the Orthodox Church. How the growth of these inchoative dogmas is brought about (by emphatically human means) we have shown above. If Mr. Nevins presses the heterodox teaching of some Fathers, yea, of Fathers who might have consulted the disciples of the Apostles, he will allow us to answer that even the very disciples of the Apostles, considered as individuals, were *fallible men*, and might have their crotchets, as well as Mr. Nevins, Cardinal Newman, and Dr. Pusey. But if, according to times and circumstances, some doctrines, though existing before, were brought out more prominently, and, as it were, as an antidote against a rising heresy, we cannot discover a trace of development in them, since no change whatever in the doctrine itself appears.

This is the chief point of misunderstanding between the East and the West. The West *develops and expands* the dogmas; the East only *states* the dogmas, and successively, by clearer expressions, *hedges out* new doubts, errors, and misrepresentations, as time goes on and sects spring up. Therefore the dogmatic growth of Rome is a growth in bulk and excrescences, which is not a sign of healthy life; whereas the *securing* of the dogmas by the Orthodox Church shows the *continuous process of an active organic life within the Orthodox Church.* Only blind people, who will not or cannot see this vital energy in Orthodoxy, call our Church *fossilised* or *petrified.* Fossils and petrifications cannot resist the doom of ages and crumble down in time; but our dogmas, preserved by the Holy Ghost, the ever-living and ever-active soul of our Church, stand forth in unfading glory and power, and will stand forth long after this world has passed away. This thought has masterly been developed by Professor Rhossis in his "*Report* (ἔκθεσις) *to the Holy Synod of the Hellenic Church concerning the last* (1875) *Union-Conference at Bonn.*" He says, p. 40: "The One Holy Catholic and Apostolic Church is a living and organic body, the Head of which is Christ, and its Soul is the Holy Ghost. . . . He (the Holy Ghost) remains for ever in the Church, leads her unto all truth, and *shapes* (διαμορφοῖ) the dogmas of her faith, her morals, her constitution (πολίτευμα), and her service. The Holy Ghost performs this *shaping* (διαμόρφωσιν) by the *formative faculty* (διὰ τῆς ἀναπλαστικῆς δυνάμεως), which He communicated to the Church, and in consequence of this faculty the Church appears throughout her historic [not dogmatic] development as living and organic body of Christ, sustained by the Holy Ghost—*always as the same.* This identity (ταὐτότης), however, does not consist in always repeating the same words, expressions, descriptions, and formulas, but in the continuous *moulding* (ἀνάπλασις) of *the same essential* (κατ' οὐσίαν) *truth.*"

We remember very well the time when Dr. Newman's "*Essay on the Development of Christian Doctrine*" appeared (1845), and what impression it made on pious and learned Roman Catholics. We were living at the time in Berlin, and had frequent intercourse with the clergy of St. Hedwig and the Roman Catholic members of the different ministerial circles, pious men, who were pillars of the Church. At that time Roman Catholicism was considerably nearer Orthodoxy than it is nowadays, and the excellent men before mentioned were a worthy aftergrowth of "*the holy family*" at Münster (Overberg, Stolberg, Fürstenberg). At first they were by Dr. Newman's book stunned as by a sudden flash of lightning. They exclaimed: "Ingenious! beautiful! but new—unheard of in the Church!

'Timeo Danaos et dona ferentes.'

Would this theory not land us in Protestantism? Would it not sanction the rationalistic tenet of *Perfectibility* of doctrine? Would it not do away with *Apostolic tradition*, on which we hitherto have based our Church? Would not the Pope, supplying history by the insidious figment of a *dormant* tradition, remain the only uncontrollable oracle of the Church?

And why did Cardinal Wiseman refuse his approbation, or (as Dr. Newman puts it) *decline* to have the book revised? Does this not look rather suspicious, as if Cardinal Wiseman was unwilling or unable to bear the responsibility for the views expressed?" Such and similar remarks were made by our friends. They did not think then that Cardinal Wiseman (excuse our calling him so by anticipation) acted *wisely;* for, whether the theory was right or wrong, the book was sure to bring shoals of Anglicans into the Roman Church; and thus the chief end was gained—increase of numbers! Keen-sighted Dr. Newman was perfectly right that Rome's position was *untenable* unless his theory was accepted. Therefore his venture was a *cardinal* stroke. However, it is still a mere theory. Khomyakoff describes Romanism as *Rationalism in the bud*, and as the true mother of Protestantism. Dr. Newman's theory is the connecting link of both the extremes, and the bridge by which the two brothers, John Henry the Ultramontane, and Francis the Unitarian, can meet. This theory is the fruit of scepticism and breeds doubt. Let us refer the reader for further information on the matter to our essays, "Cardinal J. H. Newman" (*Orthod. Cath. Review*, vol. viii. pp. 103–149), and "Religious Controversy" (*Orthod. Cath. Review*, vol. vii. pp. 72–96). Now let us hear the opinion of a man who decidedly inclines to Dr. Newman's views, and then let the reader decide for himself. W. Palmer ("*Dissertations on Subjects relating to the Orthodox Communion,*" p. 147 *seq.*) says: "Recently [Dr. Newman] has attempted in an elaborate essay not only to account for the discrepancy existing between the modern Roman and the Ancient Church, but even to turn this very discrepancy itself into an argument in favour of the Roman Communion. This he does by means of a certain theory of development, according to which the Church has power not only to enlarge her definitions of the faith by the denial of new heresies, but also to expand the faith itself by the addition of *fresh positive truths*,* the knowledge of which may have grown upon her with time from scriptural, logical, and supernatural sources, and even to contradict, it may

* The italics in the quotation are ours.

be, on some points, the confused or erroneous conceptions of earlier ages. Thus the 'Double Procession' of the Holy Spirit *may have been utterly unknown;* the Papal Supremacy may have existed *only as a dormant seed,* an *undefined* consciousness in the local Roman Church; the doctrine of the propriety of invoking saints or worshipping [we do not *worship,* but only *venerate* them] images, may have been the one unknown, the other denied; the dominant language on the subject of the state of the departed may have been inconsistent with the doctrine of Purgatory; and there may have been no other indulgences in existence but remissions of canonical penance; the doctrine of Transubstantiation, so far as the distinction of substance and accidents was concerned, may have been an open question; the Unction of the Sick may have been used chiefly for the sake of their recovery; the early history of the Blessed Virgin, and the notion of her Assumption in the Body, may have been taken from apocryphal writings, and the Fathers may have supposed that she was conceived, like the rest of mankind, with original sin: and yet, with all this, the *modern Roman doctrine* may be on all these points, by development, the true and necessary consequence, supplement, OR CORRECTION OF THE PRIMITIVE BELIEF." (P. 150): "So long as Rome seems to maintain her former antiquarian attitude towards the Eastern Church, and to dictate to her for acceptance *her own modern additions or changes,* either with unreasoning violence or on the UNTENABLE GROUND OF CONTINUOUS TRADITION, the Eastern Church may not feel herself obliged . . . to examine closely what appears *as yet only as a tolerated theory or school* within the Roman Communion. But a time will probably come when this theory, the consequences of which are too vast and important to allow of its being held in abeyance, will either be plainly and generally maintained or *rejected and condemned.*" Thus the "traditional theory," which was hitherto in general use with the Romans, and is officially still so,* is declared by Palmer to be

* The plain teaching of the Vatican Council is as follows:—"The Holy Spirit was not promised to the successors of St. Peter that by His revelation they might make known new doctrines, but that by His assistance they might inviolably

untenable and unable to justify the *modern additions to or changes in* the faith of the Roman Church. And the "development theory" is not yet authoritatively approved, and may perhaps be *rejected and condemned.* How is it then possible to base one's faith on such an uncertain ground? Then Palmer, supposing the theory of development to be received in the Roman Communion, addresses thus the Orthodox (p. 151): "There has been also one very deep cause of misunderstanding, which has never yet been properly or sufficiently acknowledged; that is, the ignorance *on both sides* of the principle and law of development—an ignorance which made us Latins, even if we were intrinsically in the right in what we sought to teach or to impose upon the whole Church, to be outwardly and apparently in the wrong, and you Greeks, even if you were intrinsically wrong in rejecting *our Latin novelties,* to be outwardly and apparently in the right; that is, according to the principle THEN [AND NOW AT THIS VERY MOMENT STILL] HELD IN COMMON ON BOTH SIDES, *that every doctrine ought to be proved by explicit and continuous tradition, and that whatever could not be proved ought to be rejected.*" Now, as the new theory is not yet authoritatively recognised, the old principle "*held in common on both sides*" is still in vigour. And by this principle, on Palmer's own showing, the Roman Church is utterly unable to justify her novelties, additions, and changes. If the truth of the Catholic Church is such a changeable thing that what we believe to-day we have to renounce to-morrow, we easily understand why Roman Catholics who leave their Church mostly cast all positive religion to the winds.* Palmer says: "We now think that

seek and faithfully expound *the deposit of faith handed down by the Apostles*" (De Eccles. iv.); and again: "The doctrine of faith which God has revealed has not been proposed like a philosophical invention, *to be perfected* by human ingenuity, but has been delivered as a divine deposit to the Bride of Christ, to be faithfully kept and infallibly declared. Hence, also, that meaning of the sacred dogmas is perpetually to be retained which our holy mother the Church has *once for all* declared; nor is that meaning ever to be departed from under the pretext of a deeper comprehension of them" (De Fide iv.) This looks uncommonly like a *rejection and condemnation* of Dr. Newman's theory.

* Read the 12th chapter of the 1st Book of Macchiavelli's *Discorsi*, and you will see how Romanism leads to infidelity. We quote from the edition 1531, issued with the *Papal privilege:* "We Italians owe to the Roman Church and her priests that, by their bad example, we have lost all religion and piety, and have become an *unbelieving* and wicked nation." And again (fol. 16): "When

the principle of *unchangeableness*, FORMERLY HELD ON ALL SIDES, was in fact *erroneous*." Thus the only theory that can save Romanism is a discovery of the nineteenth century, making its appearance a thousand years too late. And every Roman Catholic may, up to now, reject this theory. If he chooses to reject it, his ground is avowedly *untenable*, and his allegiance to the Roman Church *unreasonable* and *unjustifiable*. But if he chooses to accept it, he has to *correct the primitive belief* of his Church, *i.e.*, to acknowledge the *fallibility* of the Catholic Church. How can the Roman Catholic get out of this dilemma?

2. We do not doubt that many of our readers will agree with us in acknowledging that history furnishes abundant proofs of the schismatical character of the Church of Rome, consequently that the latter cannot claim to be the Catholic Church, the abode of the Holy Ghost, the Spirit of Truth. But many will nevertheless ask: "If the Holy Ghost has left the Roman Church, how comes it then that so many truly pious souls are found in it, and that it proves to be the way to heaven for many?" The answer is simple and easy: All those good souls who are saved *in* the Roman Church are not saved *by* the Roman but by the Orthodox Church. They belong implicitly to us, because only their *invincible ignorance* * keeps them back from us. If they were not guided by adulterated facts, if the true state of things were not concealed from them, they would also out-

---

they began to speak as potentates, and the people discovered their falsehood, men became *unbelievers*."—"Come costoro cominciarono di poi a parlare a modo de' potenti, e questa falsità si fù scoperta ne' popoli, divennero gli nomini incredoli." And a Spaniard, who has studied his country, writes in 1862 ("*Preservativo contra Roma*," p. 14): "Among the practical observations I have made on this subject, of none I feel more confident than of *the tendency of Catholicism* [Romanism] *towards infidelity*."—"Entre las observaciones prácticas que he hecho sobre esta materia, ninguna me inspira mas confianza que *la tendencia del catolicismo hácia la infidelidad*." The Romans in England are able to furnish us with some remarkable instances in this respect.

* Though Pius IX. forbids to entertain any hope of eternal salvation for all those who are not in the true Church (*Syllabus*, Prop. xvii.), and declares it as an article of faith that "nobody can be saved outside the pale of the Apostolic Roman Church," yet he declares at the same time that "*it is to be held for certain that those who labour under an invincible ignorance with respect to the true religion are free from guilt in the sight of God*."—"Ex fide est, extra Apostolicam Romanam Ecclesiam salvum fieri neminem posse . . . sed *tamen pro certo pariter habendum est, qui veræ religionis ignorantia laborent, si ea est invincibilis, nullos ipsos obstringi hujusce rei culpa ante oculos Domini*" (Allocut. Pii. IX. *Singulari quadam* de die 9 Dec. 1854). Cf. "*Lo Spirito del Cattolicismo*," per Michaelangelo Celesia, Vescovo di Patti, Roma, 1866, p. 276.

wardly join us. But now the *Index Librorum Prohibitorum* deprives them of all means to get an insight into the corruption of their Church. Therefore even priests and learned men may labour under the impediment of an invincible ignorance. Add to this the habit of education, the surroundings and associations, the family ties and bonds of friendship, and we find ample reason to excuse many excellent Roman Catholics, and many excellent Protestants too. This consideration, however, must not lead us to the conclusion that it is, after all, not essential to which Church we belong, provided we are morally good Christians. No Christian could be called good who entertained such a religious indifference and slighted Christ's one true right-believing Church. "Nobody can have God for his Father who has not the Church for his mother," says an old Father of the Church to all Christians.

Now let us turn the tables on Dr. Newman, and reproduce the wonderful passage in the 11th of his "*Lectures on Certain Difficulties felt by Anglicans in Submitting to the Catholic Church*," only taking the liberty of correcting him by changing "Roman Catholic" into "Orthodox," and "Greek" into "Roman," and making a few slight alterations besides: "A Roman Catholic country is far from being in the miserable state of a heathen population: it has portions of the truth remaining in it; it has some supernatural channels of grace; and the results are such as can never be known till we have all passed out of this visible scene of things and the accounts of the world are finally made up for the last tremendous day. While, then, I think it plain that the existence of large heterodox bodies professing Christianity are as inevitable, from the nature of the case, as infidel races or states, except under some extraordinary dispensation of divine grace—while there must ever be in the world false prophets and Antichrists by the side of the Orthodox Catholic Church,—yet it is consolatory to reflect how the schism or heresy which the self-will of a Pope or a generation has caused does not suffice altogether to destroy the work for which in some distant age evangelists have sacrificed their homes and martyrs have shed their blood. Thus the blessing is inestimable to England, so far as among us the Sacrament of Baptism is validly administered to any portion of the population. In the Roman Catholic countries, where far greater attention is paid to ritual exactness, the whole population may be considered regenerate; half the children born into the world pass from a schismatical Church to heaven, and in many of the rest it may be the foundation of a supernatural life, which is gifted with perseverance in the hour of death. There may be many who, being in invincible ignorance on those points of religion on which their Church is wrong, may have the divine unclouded illumination of faith on those numerous points on which it is right. And further, since there is a true priesthood there and a true sacrifice, the benefits of Mass to those who never had the means of knowing better may be almost the same as they are in the Orthodox Church. Humble souls who come in faith and love to the heavenly rite, under whatever disadvantages from the faulty discipline of their Communion, may obtain, as well as we, remission of such sins as the sacrifice directly effects, and that supernatural charity which wipes out the most grievous. Moreover, when the Blessed Sacrament is shown, they adore, as well as we, the true Immaculate Lamb of God; and when they communicate, it is the true Bread of Life, and nothing short of it, which they receive for the eternal health of their souls." With such eyes we look on the schismatical Roman Church.

3. The last question raised by the Romans and all the other heterodox Churches is: "If the Orthodox Church is the only true Catholic Church, why does she not say so, and come forward calling upon all Christians to join her, reclaiming them from their schism and heresy?" *This is exactly what the Orthodox Church has taught and done from the beginning of the great schism to the present day.* But the Westerns shut their eyes and stopped their ears up not to see the sign and hear the call of the Orthodox Eastern. Is there no sun because the blind cannot see it? Is there no call because the deaf cannot hear it? Does not the very word *Orthodox*, i.e., *right-believing*, imply that those who hold not the same belief are *wrong-believing*, and have there-

fore to come out and become *right-believing?* The Synod of Jerusalem (11th Decree) says: "We believe that all those, and *only those* faithful are members of the Catholic Church, who firmly hold the uncensurable (ἀμώμητον) faith of Christ the Saviour, as set forth by the same Christ and the Apostles and the holy Œcumenical Councils." Theophanes Procopovitch ("*Miscellanea Sacra,*" Breslau, 1774, p. 15) says: "We call and declare the Eastern Church *alone* to be the Church of Christ, the true, Apostolic, and Catholic Church." * And p. 64: "We dare not call you *true Christians* as long as this disagreement between us will last." † Plato, Metropolitan of Moscow, says (in his Catechism): "Our Orthodox Church is not only *the true one*, but *the only one* from the beginning of the world." [We showed above that to the Orthodox the Church is one continuous whole from Paradise to the last judgment.] Archimandrite Karpinsky, Falkovsky, Juvenal, Theophylact, Plato, Philaret, in fact, all the great luminaries of the Orthodox Church, declare that Church to be the true one, which has faithfully preserved the infallible tradition of the ancient universal Church. That this principle is the only true one is declared by Macarius, present Metropolitan of Moscow ("*Introduction à la Théologie Orthodoxe,*" Paris, 1857). He says, p. 574: "The application of this principle shows clearly the Orthodoxy of the Eastern Church and the *non-Orthodoxy of all the others.*" And p. 594: "Of all the presently existing Churches, the Orthodox Eastern Church *alone* rests on the old unchangeable basis, and *all the others* have more or less deviated from it." And p. 595: "It is a notorious fact that this (Orthodox) Church at present is *the only one* that remains faithful to the ancient Œcumenical Councils, and that, consequently, *she alone represents the true universal Church of Christ, which is infallible.*" When the Jesuit Gagarin misrepresented the Orthodox Church, a powerful writer (Karatheodory? the Eastern Mezzofanti) stood up and entirely crushed him in the book "*Orthodoxie*

---

* "*Solam* orientalem ecclesiam ecclesiam Christi, ecclesiam veram, apostolicam et catholicam appellamus et prædicamus."

"† Dicimus vos homines esse divites. . . . *Veros autem christianos,* donec quidem hæc durabit inter nos dissensio, appelare non audemus."

et Papisme," Paris, 1859. He sends the Jesuit home with a few never-to-be-forgotten lessons, which the latter ought to have learnt before leaving his mother Church, and has not yet learnt in his new Church, although the Romans in this particular entirely agree with the Orthodox. If the Jesuit thinks the Orthodox Church had not yet decided about the Roman innovations, because only an Œcumenical Council could issue such a decision, a Council composed of the East and the West, he is wrong both on Eastern and on Western principles (as the latter were still in vigour when Gagarin wrote his book, though since then they have altered); for, 1. The consent of the *ecclesia dispersa* is equivalent to the verdict of the Church assembled in Council. The voice of the infallible Church is in both cases *materially* the same. The Council only *formulates* the voice of the *ecclesia dispersa.* 2. A schismatic body is cut off from the Church, and cannot be considered an integrant part of the Church, nor a trustworthy witness to the doctrines of the Church. It can only be present at a Council as an outsider. 3. Consequently the Orthodox Church could, after the schism, at any moment have summoned an Œcumenical Council without the assistance and co-operation of the West, or rather it could not have admitted the West except on condition to return to the faith of the undivided Church. And, indeed, if the Emperor Alexander II. had not been assassinated, we should have witnessed this year an Œcumenical Council at Moscow. 4. As the voice of the *ecclesia dispersa* was hitherto sufficient to meet all the emergencies of the times, even at the time of the Reformation, the life of the Orthodox Church is manifest; but as soon as an Œcumenical Council is *needed,* and the political circumstances allow its assembling, there is not the slightest doubt that it will be convoked.

Pius IX. at the beginning of his Pontificate issued an Encyclical to the Easterns, summoning them to submit to the Roman Church. The four Patriarchs and Holy Synods sent a reply, some extracts of which we have published in the *Orthodox Catholic Review,* vol. i. pp. 234–246. This remarkable and unanswerable document is addressed to *All the Bishops everywhere.* This claim of the Orthodox Church to be the only true and Catholic Church greatly shocked the American translator, who was an Anglican Branch-Churchman. After having enumerated the divers heresies in the doctrine of the Roman Church, the Patriarchs proceed (v. 15), "That the congregations of such are also heretical, and that *spiritual communion in worship of the Orthodox sons of the Catholic Church with such is unlawful.*" The Papal Encyclical was cleverly refuted by Marcoranus, by the repentant apostate Pitzipios ("*Le Romanisme,*" Paris, 1860), Alexander Stourdza, J. Cassianus, &c. The frivolous reply to the Patriarchal Encyclical by a Mechitarist was deservedly cut to pieces by Moschatos (Athens, 1859). In the beginning he says: "In Papacy does not reign (*ἐπικρατεῖ*) the spirit of Christ, but the spirit of Satan, the spirit of lust of power, and of perversion" (*τῆς φιλαρχίας καὶ τῆς διαστροφῆς*). P. 6: "The Orthodox Church addresses to the Romans the words: 'Weep not for me, but weep for yourselves, and for your children.'" Staurides in a "*Dialogue of an Orthodox and a Papist,*" Vienna, 1862, says: "The term Catholic Church signified and signifies chiefly the ancient and genuine Church, such as at present *only the Eastern* happens to be (*ὁποία σήμερον μόνον ἡ ἀνατολικὴ τυγχάνει οὖσα*). Another Orthodox writes: (*Εὐαγγελικὸς κῆρυξ* Sept. 1857, p. 401): "Only the Orthodox Eastern Church is the true one, and *without her there is no salvation*" (*ἐκτὸς δὲ ταύτης οὐδεμία ὑπάρχει σωτηρία*). These proofs will be sufficient to dispel the Western ignorance about the claims of the Orthodox Church to be the true Catholic Church, *to the exclusion of all others.* Consequently it is *the duty* of all outsiders to join her. If the West listens to her voice, she must resuscitate our old ante-schismatical Western Church, so that we might reconquer the schismatic territory and heal the divisions of Christendom. The Catholic-minded Anglicans and the Westerns generally, though they have been estranged for a thousand years, have not quite forgotten their Eastern mother Church. They have learnt by sad experience what Rome is, and yearn for the East.

EX ORIENTE LUX!

Holy Scripture denounces *schism* and *heresy* as a great evil to be avoided by all Christians (1 Cor. i. 10, xii. 25, xi. 19; Tit. iii. 10.) As the Apostles taught, so taught their disciples. St. Ignatius (*Ep. ad Philadelph.* 3) says: "If any man follows him that makes a schism (σχίζοντι) in the Church, *he shall not inherit the kingdom of God.*" And in his Epistle to the *Trallians*, chap. vi.: "I . . . entreat you that ye use Christian nourishment only, and abstain from herbage of a different kind; I mean *heresy*. For those [that are given to this] mix up Jesus Christ with *their own poison*, speaking things which are unworthy of credit, like *those who administer a deadly drug in sweet wine*, which he who is ignorant of does greedily take, with a fatal pleasure, *leading to his own death.*" This is the doctrine of the Apostle St. John, as he taught it his disciple St. Ignatius, and his disciple St. Polycarp, and St. Polycarp taught it St. Irenæus, who writes (*Advers. Hæres.* lib. iii. cap. iii. note 4): "He [Polycarp] it was who, coming to Rome in the time of Anicetus, caused many to turn away from the aforesaid heretics to the Church of God, proclaiming that he had received this one and sole truth from the Apostles—that, namely, which is handed down by the Church. There are also those who heard from him that John, the disciple of the Lord, going to bathe at Ephesus, and perceiving Cerinthus within, rushed out of the bath-house without bathing, exclaiming, 'Let us fly, lest even the bath-house fall down, because Cerinthus, the enemy of the truth, is within.' And Polycarp himself replied to Marcion, who met him on one occasion, and said, 'Dost thou know me?' 'I do know thee, *the first-born of Satan.*' *Such was the horror which the Apostles and their disciples had against holding even a verbal communication with any corrupters of the truth;* as Paul also says, 'A man that is an heretic, after the first and second admonition, *reject;* knowing that he that is such is subverted and sinneth, *being condemned of himself.*'" Here is Apostolic teaching! Here is Apostolic *horror of schism and heresy!*

But what do we see in the Anglican Church? Heresies are not only tolerated and publicly preached from the pulpits, and the schismatical and heretical Church of Rome is by a great many fondled and looked up to, but a theory has sprung up, the so-called *Branch-Church theory*, maintaining that the Catholic Church consists of three branches: the Roman, Greek, and Anglican Churches. Only fancy! the Roman and Greek Churches *contradicting and anathematising each other*, and the Anglican Church (in its Articles) *contradicting both*, and besides full of heretical teaching—these are the component parts of the One Catholic Church, *the abode of the Spirit of Truth!!!* And on this theory rests the "*Corporate Reunion of Christendom*," which entirely ignores all Apostolic teaching concerning schism and heresy!

Both Churches, the Orthodox and the Roman, agree in teaching that a *schismatic body* is cut off from the one true Catholic Church, and forms no longer part of *the mystical body of Christ*. Such a body may have *valid* Sacraments —as an inheritance from the Apostles—but their use is *irregular and unlawful*, so that any one who is aware of the schismatical character of the respective Church *sins* when he administers or receives a Sacrament in that Church; *e.g.*, if an Orthodox receives the Communion in a Roman Church, he receives it unworthily, because he enters thereby into communion with a schismatical Church, which is a grievous sin. Such a schismatic Church has *no jurisdiction*, no *lawful* Bishops. The Pope is a Bishop, indeed, in consequence of his ordination, but he is neither Bishop *of Rome* nor *Patriarch of the West*, but an intruder "who entereth not by the door into the sheepfold, but climbeth up some other way; the same is a thief and a robber."

The Anglican Church, being a daughter of the Roman Church, naturally participated in *Rome's schism*. When Henry VIII. separated, he threw off, indeed, the yoke of the Pope, but did not alter the Church besides, and it remained *schismatic*. When Edward VI. altered the Anglican Church by infusing Protestant blood into the same, he abolished Roman heresies, but introduced Protestant heresies instead. Thus the schism remained the same. But even if the Anglican Church had done away with all the Roman heresies, and had adopted all the

Orthodox dogmas, it would still have been a *schismatical* Church; for since the bond of Catholic unity had been *visibly* disjointed, it must, of necessity, be *visibly* re-conjoined. An *invisible* or *spiritual* union is unavailable in a *visible* Church. In this respect the Protestant notion of an invisible Church is so strong in the Anglicans, that even the most advanced Churchmen, who emphatically inculcate the visibility of the Church, all at once turn Invisibilists as soon as they have to face the question whether it is their duty or not to join *visibly* that Church which they have found to be the true one. It is a characteristic of Protestantism to make light of schism and heresy. This characteristic is prominent in the Anglican Church. Nobody denies that Calvinism and Rationalism are preached *freely and with impunity* throughout the length and breadth of the Anglican Church. Nobody denies that the Ancient Church, on the contrary, jealously watched the purity of the Catholic faith, and convened Œcumenical Councils to expel the heretical poison from the body of the Church, in order to keep the latter sound and safe. Yet the most orthodox-minded Anglicans are satisfied to remain in Church-communion with the heretic members of their Church. This wonderful phenomenon is unaccountable except on the supposition that Protestantism has eaten into the very heart of the Anglicans, whatever shades of opinion they may hold besides. To remain in the Anglican Church in order to *un-Protestantise* it, as Dr. Pusey pretends to do, would be tantamount to remaining in the flames of a burning house in order to save the inmates. Must he not come out, and bring the others out, or perish in the flames? The Holy Ghost, the Spirit of Truth, decidedly cannot dwell in a Church where heresy is tolerated. If Dr. Pusey points to the fruits of the Spirit visible in the Anglican Church as a proof that the Anglican Church, in spite of the heresies within her pale, is a living branch of the Catholic Church, he is greatly mistaken. Let him look round, and he will find in every Church or sect such fruits of the Spirit, in some more, in others less. These fruits of the Spirit are wrought by Him in the souls of those Christians who, though in consequence of *ignorantia invincibilis* being without the true Church, are *implicitly* members of the Orthodox Catholic Church. If some Anglicans make a distinction between *Establishment* and *Church*, in order to relegate the heresies to the Establishment and clear their Church, the expedient fails, since nobody can trace the line of demarcation.

Let us, by all means, have the Christianity of Christ and the Apostles, though the present age may think it clumsy, uncouth, superstitious, and uncharitable. Let us not have that highly clarified decoction of "fashionable nineteenth century Christianity," so refined and tender-hearted, so charitable and comprehensive, that it not only includes all Christian sects, but embraces Reform-Jews, Mohammedans, Parsees, and Brahmos. Anglican Bishops boast of the *comprehensiveness* of their Church, and ignore the ill-assorted elements in the same, commending *religious indifference*, and, though unconsciously, colluding with *growing infidelity*. Truth is essentially *exclusive*, i.e., *intolerant of error*. Truth cannot overlook or make light of error for peace's sake. Therefore Jeremiah (vi. 14) says: "They heal the wounds of my people slightly, saying, Peace, peace; when there is no peace" [so the Hebrew text]; "Behold, for peace they have great bitterness" (Isa. xxxviii. 17); "Thus saith the Lord, Stand ye in the ways, and see, and *ask for the old paths, where is the good way, and walk therein, and ye shall find rest for your souls*" (Jer. vi. 16). Truth *must* combat error wherever she finds it. She must not connive at error, must not go hand in hand with it; for "what communion hath light with darkness?" (2 Cor. vi. 14). If she would act thus, she would already have passed into the stage of *indifference*, and begin to doubt of its own existence, asking, with Pilate, "What is truth?" This indifference is the basis of "*Corporate Reunion*" as opposed to "*Individual Secession*." Is, then, the individual quietly to remain in a Church, which he knows to be wrong, till the rest of his fellow-Churchmen think it convenient to leave it? Has the individual no responsibility in the sight of God? Can he with an easy mind push his responsibility from his own shoulders on a corrupted Church? If he was born into such a Church, can it be an excuse for remaining in it, since God has given him eyes to distinguish light from darkness?

The Anglo-Catholics will have nothing to do with Protestantism, nor will they leave the Anglican Church either. WE AGREE WITH THEM. Do not listen to the siren's voice of Rome. Your *present* Church is, of course, corrupted and schismatic. Therefore the Tractarians went back to the pre-Reformation Church. However, that Church was also schismatic. Why will you not go a few centuries farther back, to the Seventh Œcumenical Council of the Undivided Church? There is the undoubted Catholic Church, of which Rome herself was a part—a Church without schism and heresy. Let us refer the reader for further information to our paper, "*The True Old English Church*" (*Orthod. Cath. Review*, vol. ix. pp. 1–14). If the Anglicans go back to the period indicated, the Orthodox will recognise them as their legitimate brethren, and the Catholic bond, torn asunder by the Roman schism, will be *visibly* tied again. Therefore we do not say, with Rome, "*Secede!*" but "*Return!*" Return to *your old home, your good old English home;* let the Latins go their way; keep your own language, rites, and customs, as you had them in the days of yore, before you bent your neck under the Papal yoke!

The Anglicans will naturally wish to know the opinion of the Orthodox Church with respect to their Orders. She declares them neither invalid (as the Roman does) nor valid, but, since that degree of certainty is wanting which is absolutely necessary in a Sacrament, she reordains the priests who join her. We will not examine the historical part of the question, but Anglicans generally overlook that it has also a dogmatical part. There is an element in the English Church which materially affects our subject. The majority of Anglicans are Protestant in belief, and the Episcopal bench consists (with very few exceptions) exclusively of Low and Broad Churchmen. Now, it is a curious fact that of all the Protestant Episcopal Churches not a single one has Orders recognised by the Orthodox Church, though, *e.g.*, the Moravians derive their Episcopate from an apostate Greek Bishop. (The consecration by one Bishop, though *irregular*, is undoubtedly *valid.*) Is there perhaps anything in the very substance of Protestantism which prevents the Orthodox Church from recognising Orders administered by Protestants? Yes; there is something in the Protestant doctrine that hollows the Catholic notion of priesthood as *qualitativè* distinct from laity,—something that undermines the Catholic notion of hierarchy, so as to leave nothing but the bare name and title of a merely honorary rank. This something is the doctrine, common to all Protestant Churches, and insisted upon by the Anglican Low Church (fiercely denouncing Sacramentalism in any shape),—the doctrine of *the general priesthood* of all the faithful. They say: *Only for order's and convenience's sake* certain men were separated for the work of the ministry. They had no special divine powers conferred upon them in a sacramental way. Every layman had the same powers, though he was expected, for order's sake, not to use them. The general priesthood, this central doctrine of Protestantism, destroys the belief in a privileged order of priests and bishops. Where the names were still retained, the original substance and significance of these names were irretrievably gone. Have the Anglican Articles of Religion, framed by avowed Protestants, the slightest hint at the *sacerdotal* character of priesthood? *Priest* was to them not ἱερεὺς, but simply πρεσβύτερος, or *elder*. *Bishop* was to them not "the summit of the priesthood" (ἡ ἀκμὴ τῆς ἱερωσύνης), but simply a *superintendent* or *overseer*. Where such notions prevail, *there is no certainty of the conscientious observance of all that is considered by the Orthodox Catholic Church as necessary to a valid administration of the Sacrament of Orders.* If Orthodox Bishops (or any heretical Bishops whose Orders are recognised as valid by the Orthodox Church) join the Protestant Church and ordain priests and bishops, fulfilling all that is requisite and necessary in the eyes of the Orthodox Church to make the ordination *valid*, there is no doubt that such clergymen would be recognised by the Orthodox Church as *valid* (though not as legitimate) priests and bishops, and no reordination would or could be demanded on their joining the Orthodox Church. If, however, the very idea of a sacerdotal priesthood is lost, how is it reasonably to be expected that the bishops will scrupulously stick to the *forma et materia sacramenti* as required by the Orthodox Church in ordaining bishops, priests, and deacons? We are prepared to hear the Anglicans answer, "Our Bishops are not allowed to deviate from the forms of ordaining bishops, priests, and deacons as prescribed in the Prayer-Book; thus all surety required is given. Examine these forms, and you are safe in judging our Orders." Are, indeed, the Anglican Bishops and clergy such strict and conscientious observers of what the Prayer-Book prescribes? The Anglo-Catholics have another tale to tell about this. Do they not complain, week after week, of their Low Church Bishops and clergy disregarding the injunctions of the Prayer-Book? But let us hear what the great Anglican authority, the "judicious" Hooker, says: "The whole Church visible being the true and original subject of all power, it hath not *ordinarily* allowed any other than bishops alone to ordain; howbeit, as the ordinary course in all things is ordinarily to be observed, so *it may be in some cases necessary that we decline from the ordinary ways.*" If Bishop Cosins took repeatedly the Lord's Supper in Presbyterian churches, he must have cared little whether a minister was a validly ordained priest or not. And Bishop Hall (who is found in Dr. Pusey's Catena) explicitly states respecting the episcopal character of the English Church: "We ALL profess this form *not to be essential* to the being of a Church." You see the English Church offers scarcely better guarantees for the preservation of valid orders than any other Protestant Episcopal Church.

Now we have to explain some Orthodox doctrines which are a sore trial and a stumbling-block to most Anglicans, even to those who are otherwise well disposed towards the Orthodox Church—doctrines the denial of which shows how deeply Protestantism has eaten into the flesh of the Anglican body, and how the show of Catholic appearance is more specious than real. These doctrines are the *Invocation of Saints*, and *the cultus of Icons and Relics.* It is a pity that such a wild Protestant invective against these doctrines in

Dr. Littledale's "*Plain Reasons against Joining the Church of Rome*" should bear the name of a man whom we esteemed almost as our fellow-Churchman, but who is, as we now know, a thorough and genuine Protestant, and a bitter Protestant too. Dr. Littledale, who in his former books reverentially spoke of the "*Holy*" Eastern Church, now stigmatises the Seventh Œcumenical Council of the "*Decrepit*" Eastern Church. If this is a progress in the right direction, we may expect to see some more doctrines fall by and by.

Let us begin by examining the Orthodox doctrine respecting the *Cultus of Icons* or holy pictures. It is a known fact that *graven images* are not allowed in the Orthodox Church. Thus, strictly speaking, we cannot contravene the Second Commandment. But the burden of the Commandment was by no means contained in the word "*graven*," but in the prohibition of making an image *of the Deity*. Döllinger expresses this beautifully ("*Heidenthum und Judenthum*," p. 805). In Exod. xx. 4, 5, and Deut. v. 8, not a word is said that absolutely forbade the Israelites to make a picture or image, except one of God for the purpose of worshipping Him in this figure or symbolic representation. Opposite heathenism, which constantly drew God down into Nature and bodily mixed Him up with it, Jehovah was to be known and worshipped by the Hebrews as the Invisible One who had no palpable and decaying figure, but rather was totally distinct from the world. And the longer Russian Catechism says: "We are forbidden [in the Second Commandment] to bow down to graven images or idols, as to supposed deities, or as to likenesses of false gods." That images generally were forbidden is a fiction of the Iconoclasts. Was it not God Himself who commanded two Cherubim to be made overshadowing the mercy-seat (*capporeth*)? Was it not God Himself who "called by name" Bezaleel and Aholiab, and filled them "with the spirit of God, in wisdom, and in understanding, and in knowledge, and in all manner of workmanship, to devise cunning works, to work in gold, and in silver, and in brass, . . . and in carving of timber, to work in all manner of workmanship"? (Exod. xxxi. 1–6). Thus no Christian can object to the images of the Cherubim in the Holy of Holies, because God Himself ordered, and even (in a certain sense) designed them, by inspiring Bezaleel and Atholiab; yet they seem to be rather inconvenient to the taste and argument of Dr. Littledale, for (l. c. p. 26) he adds to the words: "The figures of the Cherubim in the Holy of Holies" this significant remark: "Where, however, only one man ever saw them, and that only once a year." But we ask, Was the *principle* of making images right or wrong? Was it wrong?—then not even a single man once a year is allowed to face it. Was it right?—then all the people may witness it. The Cherubim were not (as Dr. Littledale seems to imply) removed from the gaze of the people because they might have been made objects of idolatry, but because they were connected with the mercy-seat and the *Shechinah*, this typical *Mystery*, foreshadowing the N. T. Real Presence in the Holy Eucharist. If the Cherubim were dangerous for the people to look at, why did the Lord not hesitate to command Moses: "Make thou a fiery serpent, and set it upon a pole: and it shall come to pass that every one that is bitten, when he looketh upon it, shall live"? (Num. xxi. 8). How could such an image have a healing power? Was the *brass* perhaps endued with such a wonderful quality? St. John iii. 14, 15, reveals to us the secret: "As Moses lifted up the serpent in the wilderness, even so must the Son of Man be lifted up, that whosoever *believeth* in Him should not perish, but have eternal life." Here you have exactly the doctrine of the Orthodox Church respecting the cultus of Icons. Such Icons are, indeed, more than simply an historical representation, a sort of painted sermon. They are made for the purpose that the faithful may *pray before them*, as the Israelites had prayerfully to *look upon* the serpent. And as the Israelites were not saved by the brazen figure, but *by the Great Physician of our souls, Jesus Christ*, whose atoning death on the cross and final victory over the serpent in Paradise was prefigured in Moses's serpent on the pole: so also the minds of the Orthodox are to be lifted up by faith from the picture before them to *the only source of all grace, Jesus Christ, our High Priest.* If the picture represents the Blessed Virgin, the Apostles, or other saints, our minds and prayers have not to abide with them, but *to ascend with them* to the throne of grace of Him from whom *alone* come all good gifts. Here the Iconoclasts will say: "If we can do without Icons and need not such frail crutches to approach our God, why should we use them?" We have no doubt a free approach to God, and so had the Israelites; yet God wished them, in this particular case, to apply to Him by means of the brazen serpent. Why? They did not know at the time, but Christ declared to us His Father's deep counsel. The Orthodox Church, the organ of the Holy Ghost, declares to us that the proper use of Icons is most salutary to us? Why? Partly because it is a necessary supplement to the doctrine of the Invocation of Saints, as we shall see hereafter. The full reason why we shall see when all veils are removed and we see Him face to face.

Now let us proceed to Christian Church history. In the beginning of the Christian Church the use of pictures was naturally restricted, though by no means in abeyance, as the safe hiding-places of the Catacombs show, in which we saw ourself plenty of pictures, reaching back as far as the beginning of the second century. The oldest picture we remember is in the Cemetery of St. Priscilla, and represents the Holy Virgin with Child, very much like our traditional Icons, with a prophet (Isa. vii.?) pointing to her. It is painted on the wall and much dilapidated, but fully recognisable. The Christian churches, or rather private houses used as churches, which were exposed to the attack of heathens, did not display anything that might arouse the suspicions of heathens or betray their religion. Therefore an outsider, on entering such a church, would find nothing, no altar, no cross, no picture. The table (*mensa*, *τράπεζα*) was their altar. The heathen *ara*, *βωμὸς* was an abomination to them. The heathen *altare* was a vessel fitting to the *ara*, and placed on the top of it for the use of burnt-offerings, as Quintilian informs us (*aris altaria imponere*), consequently not less objectionable to the mind of a Christian than an *ara*. It would have been very unwise to attract the attention of enemies by the exhibition of pictures, which do not form an essential part of the divine service. And crosses? They could easily hide them, for they were undeniably used by the Christians, generally used, and more extensively used than in the present day; in fact, so much so, that the heathens called the Christians *Cross-worshippers*. If Dr. Littledale had attended to this fact, if he had attended to the drift of the treatises from which the passages produced are taken, he could easily have refuted himself. The bare quotation of patristic passages is of no more value than the string of Bible texts in support of some heresy. Both require a closer inspection. We wonder that the Carpocratians are brought forward as witnesses against us, since they were *heathens*, nothing else, as St. Irenæus (Adv. hær. i. 25, 1), St. Hippolytus (Refutat. omnium hæres. vii. 32), and St. Epiphanius (Hær. xxvii. 2) distinctly state. They believed Christ to be simply the son of Joseph and Mary. The Fathers noticed them only because they adopted a Christian veil, borrowed from the Gnostics, for their religious system. St. Hippolytus (l. c.) says that they believed that those who despised the world-making Archons, as Jesus did, had the *same* power as Jesus, and some were *still mightier* (δυνατωτέρους) than Jesus. Consequently, what can their mode of image-worship concern us? However, St. Irenæus does not say a word against the veneration of Christian images, but only mentions Carpocratian "honouring these images *after the same manner as the Gentiles*." The quotation of Minucius Felix is most interesting and instructive. Has Dr. Littledale perhaps read the beginning of the chapter from which he quotes? If so, he would have seen what sort of crosses we *neither worship nor wish for*. There we read: "For in that you attribute to our religion *the worship of a criminal and his cross*, you wander far from the neighbourhood of the truth in thinking either that a criminal deserved, or that an earthly being was able, *to be believed God*." Now let the reader consult "Tertullian's Apologeticus," cp. 16, and he will see how both writers are dependent on each other. Both were contemporaries, both lived (at least for a time) in Rome, both were most likely countrymen of Africa. Tertullian shows still more fully that the heathens called the Christians Cross-worshippers (*crucis religiosos*), because they believed them to worship the cross *as an idol.* Tertullian sarcastically says (l. c.): "Then if any of you think us worshippers of the cross, in that adoration he is sharer with us. If you *propitiate* a piece of wood, it matters little what it is like when the substance is the same: the form is of no consequence, if you have *the very body of the God*" (*ipsum dei corpus*). Does it not strike our readers how the Christians could ever have been called Cross-worshippers, if not a certain *lawful cultus of the cross* had existed, which the heathens misinterpreted? If the Iconoclasts reply: "Such a conclusion is hasty, since the Christians were also called Ass-worshippers without the slightest reason," Tertullian fully and satisfactorily answers them in the first part of the chapter, and in his book "Ad Nationes," cap. xi. As to Dr. Littledale's quotations from Origen, they are not more to the point than the preceding ones; in fact, they treat the same subject, *i.e.*, images worshipped as gods, or heathen idolatry. No Orthodox *addresses lifeless objects*, but the living originals in heaven. No Orthodox *offers to images his prayers,* though he may pray *before* them, using the painted representation as a means to bring the original before his mind. But Origen is most decidedly wrong in saying: "What sensible man can refrain from smiling when he sees that one . . . imagines *that by gazing on these natural things he can ascend from the visible symbol to that which is spiritual and immaterial?*" For what purpose were, then, symbols given in the Old Testament and parables in the New Testament? Was it not to lead men from the visible to the invisible, from the corporeal to the spiritual? Has Dr. Littledale taken the trouble of reading the whole 19th chapter of the second book of the "Divine Institutions" by Lactantius? How can he then seriously produce against us a passage so plainly speaking of *heathen* image-worship, which is a totally different thing from the Christian veneration of images? What can there be more telling than this passage of the same chapter?—"For this is the state of the case, that whosoever shall prostrate his soul, which has its origin from heaven, to the *infernal* and lowest things (*ad inferna et ima prostraverit*), must fall to that place to which he has cast himself." This clearly points to the opinion, shared by all the primitive Fathers, that the heathen idols were possessed by the devils or were organs of the demons. Next the 36th Canon of the Council of Elvira is quoted. But let us first hear something about this Council. It was composed of *nineteen* Bishops, the names of whom are given (though one Codex puts the number forty-three, however without giving the additional names). The Acts mark its date 324. But Hosius of Corduba, who figures among its members, was at that time not in Spain, but was already in 323 at the Imperial Court in Nicomedia, and lived from 323 to 325 partly in Nicomedia, partly in Alexandria and Nicæa. No wonder that Berardi and Molkenbuhr (an eminent canonist of Münster) doubt of the genuineness of the Acts. Moreover, the first Canon is plainly tainted with the Novatian error. Dr. Littledale can now estimate at its true value the weight of such a Council. However, even apart from these considerations, the 36th Canon seems to be a fruit of the persecution of Diocletian, and of the desire to avoid anything that could betray the persecuted Christians. That we must either sacrifice the Council or assign a much earlier date to it is quite clear from the above remarks. Moreover, the few words of the Canon do not state whether *all* pictures, or only the mysteries, *e.g.*, the Holy Trinity, were forbidden. If we decide for "*all*," the Canon is apparently at variance with the general practice of the Church, as we shall hear presently. Dr. Littledale next quotes "Eusebius's Church History," vii. 14; but as this is a misquotation, we tried to find out its source, and found it in the book, "What is Romanism?" published by the same Society by which his book "Plain Reasons," &c., is published. "What is Romanism?" is a series of twenty-six tracts, and forms a rich storehouse for any one who wishes to attack the Roman and (partly at least) the Orthodox Church. In the 23d tract, p. 32, we find almost the same wording of the translation and the same misquotation, cap. 14 instead of 18. It is certainly "bookmaking made easy;" but whether it is the safest and most creditable way is another question. The passage of Eusebius is worthless for our purpose, since only the worship of Christian images *by heathens*, of course according to their idolatrous heathen custom, is mentioned.

The fact of St. Epiphanius tearing a curtain up in a church at Anablatha because a picture was painted on it, "contrary to the authority of the Scriptures and contrary to our religion," must seem conclusive to our opponents. But a little more knowledge of Church history and of Patrology soon turns the scales. Who was St. Epiphanius? "A saint and great scholar." No doubt he was, for, besides being a great linguist, his intentions were pure. He was very zealous, but at the same time very *indiscreet* and *injudicious;* very learned, but *by no means reliable* (as R. A. Lipsius in his book "*Zur Quellen-Kritik des Epiphanios,*" Wien, 1865, has fully shown); impulsive and passionate, carried away by the inspiration of the moment, even beyond the sacred boundaries of the Holy Canons; in short, harsh and absolute in his measures. Such a man was Epiphanius. No wonder that his life was a checkered career. What business had Epiphanius to act in the church at Anablatha as if he was the master of the house? He ought to have appealed to the Diocesan, and we should most likely have heard a very different verdict (as our illustration from St. Basil will show). And what shall we say about his open defiance of the Holy Canons by ordaining St. Jerome's brother Paulinianus priest? And Socrates, vi. 12–14, and Sozomenus, viii. 14, 15, tell us how he disregarded St. Chrysostom, and acted at Constantinople as if he were in his own diocese. Epiphanius's act at Anablatha was far from being approved by other Orthodox people, for Epiphanius himself, in his letter to John, Bishop of Jerusalem, says: "I have heard that *some complain against me,* because . . . " and then he recounts the incident at Anablatha. The letter referred to is only preserved in St. Jerome's translation, and would most likely have been ignored by Jerome had it not been for the smart hit against Origen (and consequently against Rufinus) at the end of the letter, too great a temptation for Jerome's pugnacious mind to be resisted.

Now let us shift the scene in a northerly direction and betake ourselves to Neo-Cæsarea, where on the 14th June 370 St. Basil succeeded to Eusebius on the archiepiscopal throne. Three years before (367) St. Epiphanius became

Bishop of Salamis (Constantia), in the island of Cyprus. Thus both were contemporaries. Epiphanius no doubt belongs to Dr. Littledale's "*Holy*" Eastern Church, but Basil, *one of the greatest Saints and Doctors of the Orthodox Church*, belongs to Dr. Littledale's "*Decrepit*" Eastern Church, for he teaches exactly the doctrine which in 787 the Seventh Œcumenic Council at Nicæa proclaimed, when "the Eastern Church had entered on its decrepitude" ("*Plain Reasons*," p. 36). Here are St. Basil's words (Epist. 360 *ad Julian Apostat.*, in Opp. tom. iii. p. 463, ed. Maur.): "Whence I honour and *do obeisance to* the features of their pictures (Icons), particularly because they have been *handed down from [the time of] the Holy Apostles, and have not been forbidden, but are represented in* ALL *our churches.*" *Ὅθεν καὶ τοὺς χαρακτῆρας τῶν εἰκόνων αὐτῶν τιμῶ καὶ προςκυνῶ, κατ' ἐξαίρετον τούτων παραδεδομένων ἐκ τῶν ἁγίων ἀποστόλων, καὶ οὐκ ἀπηγορευμένων, ἀλλ' ἐν πάσαις ταῖς ἐκκλησίαις ἡμῶν τούτων ἀνιστορουμένων.*

Let us add a few explanatory remarks. The Greek *προςκυνεῖν* (like the Hebrew *hishtachavah*) is used with regard to both God and creatures, and means "to prostrate one's self before another" in token of respect, "to kiss the hand or do obeisance to anybody," as sign of veneration. It is, therefore, the *inward* act of veneration accompanied by an *outward* sign. St. Basil uses both verbs, *τιμᾶν* (to honour) and *προσκυνεῖν*, in order to show that the veneration is not to be understood of divine worship, which is expressed by the word *λατρεία*. In the same way the Seventh Œcumenical Council calls this veneration *τὴν τιμητικὴν προσκύνησιν*. In order to mark the difference by single words, the Church adopted the term *Doulia* (*δουλεία*) for the cultus of Saints (*hyperdoulia* for the Blessed Virgin), because that term never at any time was used of divine worship.* *Latria* was an old term for divine worship, used as such by the heathen. "*Their* pictures" refers to "apostles, prophets, and

* The *verb δουλεύω* (like the Hebrew *abad*) is certainly also used of divine worship, but we are not aware of *a single passage* of the Old and New Testament in which the *substantive δουλεία* and the correspondent Hebrew "*aboda*" were used in this sense. And the reason why they were not used appears from Rom. viii. 15; "For ye received not the spirit of *bondage* (*δουλείας*) again unto

martyrs" in the text preceding our quotation. "Handed down from the Apostles." What can there be plainer? Or shall we suppose that Dr. Littledale knows better than St. Basil what Apostolic tradition is? St. Epiphanius, brought up in anchoretical seclusion with St. Hilarion, might have known little of the splendour of Christian temples and their Icons. An ascetic rigour and austere simplicity are features of his character. "And have not been forbidden." This seems to imply that contradiction in some quarters had been raised, as every Christian dogma has met with contradiction. But how unavailing this contradiction was we see from the concluding words, that Icons "are represented in ALL our churches."

It would simply be waste of time to scan Dr. Littledale's quotations from St. Ambrose and St. Augustine, as they are quite beside the mark, as even a superficial reader will perceive. And as to Serenus, the first Iconoclast, Dr. Littledale may justly anticipate that the majority of his readers will side with Pope St. Gregory the Great, who abhors not less the divine worship of images than the Orthodox Church always did, and still does up to the present day. The Decree (ὅρος) of the Seventh Œcumenical Council expressly says: "The honour shown to the Icon refers to the original, and he who venerates the Icon venerates in it the person of the one who is represented." *Ἡ γὰρ τῆς εἰκόνος τιμὴ ἐπὶ τὸ πρωτότυπον διαβαίνει, καὶ ὁ προσκυνῶν τὴν εἰκόνα προσκυνεῖ ἐν αὐτῇ τοῦ ἐγγραφομένου τὴν ὑπόστασιν.* Therefore the Council permits only the *veneration* (*τὴν τιμητικὴν προσκύνησιν*) of images, and restricts the *adoration* proper (*τὴν ἀληθινὴν λατρείαν*) to God.

If Dr. Littledale had read Hefele's "*Concilien-Geschichte*" vol. iii. pp. 410–454 and pp. 646–671, he would better appreciate the Seventh Œcumenical Council, signed by the Papal Legates, who fully agreed with the Decree (Hefele, l. c. p.

---

fear; but ye received the spirit of adoption." And Gal. iv. 24: ". . . . these women are two covenants; one from mount Sinai, bearing children unto *bondage* (εἰς δουλείαν) . . . (v. 26). But the Jerusalem that is above is *free*, which is our mother." Therefore St. Paul (Rom. xii. 1) requires of the Christians a "reasonable *worship* (λατρείαν)."

436); and he would know how the Fathers of the Council of Frankfurt in 794 were deceived by falsified acts, in which προσκυνεῖν was constantly translated "*adorare*," so that the Fathers rejected *exactly the same thing that the Council of Nicæa rejected.* The reader may judge how shamefully the Fathers of Frankfort were duped by the supposititious Acts of the Seventh Œcumenical Council, as they were lying before them; for the second of the fifty-six *capitula*, which the Frankfurt Synod set up, maintains that the Nicene Council anathematised all those who did not offer to the pictures of the Saints *the same service and adoration as to the Holy Trinity* (Hefele, l. c. p. 646). Did Dr. Littledale know this? If so, why did he not inform the reader? If not, why did he not inform himself before judging so important a matter in such an offhand way? And as to the œcumenicity of our Nicene Council, Dr. Littledale (quite seriously) argues, p. 36: "It never has had the acceptance by Christendom which is necessary to make a Council rank as general and binding, nor can it ever acquire it now." Did Dr. Littledale not know that the East *and the West* recognised it as an Œcumenical Council from 787 to the present day? The Council of Frankfurt rejected, *not our Council of Nicæa, but an imaginary Council*, and the single dissentient voices down to the fourteenth century shared the wrong impression produced by the Council of Frankfort. The present Roman Church recognises our second Council of Nicæa as œcumenical (as Cardinal Manning can inform Dr. Littledale), and no proof can be produced that Rome ever authoritatively rejected it. Or can Dr. Littledale mark a time, later that 787, when Rome began to recognise our Council? Beside the study of Hefele, we should advise Dr. Littledale to read Dr. Michaud's excellent book "*Discussion sur les Sept Conciles œcuméniques*," Berne, 1878. Here he will find that the opinion on the *libri Carolini* was the same in the East and in the West, *with the solitary exception of "some Anglicans of a certain party, who seem to have made it their speciality to attack the œcumenicity of this seventh Council in any and every way, and to discredit it* per fas et nefas *by imputing to it a doctrine which it has never taught*" (p. 301).

Then from pp. 301–305 he refutes Mr. Meyrick in a truly masterly way.

God endowed man with *imagination*, and as this faculty is His gift, He wished it to be appreciated and employed in the right way. Images are the *instruments* our imagination works with. Therefore they cannot be bad if employed in the right way. In fact, the corporeo-spiritual constitution of man cannot do without them. If we were angels we might dispense with them. The Puritan hatred of images was unreasonable barbarity. Every one of us knows how deeply the veneration of images is seated in human nature. Have you a likeness of a departed parent or friend of whom you were affectionately fond? Did you never contemplate it tenderly and with emotions suggestive of love and admiration, and of a virtuous resolve to be worthy of their love? In short, have you never been carried away by your feelings beyond the dead lineaments on the paper or canvas to the living original? Would you assign a place of honour to such a picture, or would you not mind throwing it on a heap of rubbish? Why should you treat this picture differently from the rest? There is no intrinsic value, no magic power hidden in it. Now, if a likeness of a friend of yours is so precious to you, ought not a likeness or representation of a friend of God to be infinitely more precious to us? Can we be reproached with showing all signs of tender love and humble supplication (addressed to the original and not to the dead materials, which were only instrumental in reminding us of the original) to those who are round the throne of God? If we fall down before a friend, beseeching him to assist us in great distress or to help us by his prayer, do we act as heathens or idolaters? Or do you think that the perfected saints round the throne of God are less powerful in pleading for us, or more indifferent as to our salvation than our imperfect brethren here below? And as to the use of burning lamps before the Icons and offering incense to them, every liturgical scholar knows that these are symbolic actions, denoting that the saints wish us to let our light shine before the whole world in faith and good works, and that our prayer to them and their prayer for us may ascend like sweet-smelling incense to the throne of God. No man in his senses will dare to assert that the Orthodox believe that the kissing, bowing, lights, and incense are meant for the wooden tablet called Icon. It happened more than once that a Bishop, seeing an undue reverence paid to an Icon, destroyed it, as "Hezekiah brake in pieces the brazen serpent that Moses had made." Archbishop Alexander Lycurgos did so not many years ago. But, you will ask, can it be denied that there are Orthodox who act as if they ascribed a certain undefinable magic power to Icons, or wear crosses and pictures as heathens wear amulets? We are sorry that there are such superstitious people; but how can the Church be made responsible for what she does *not* teach? Superstition is apt to creep in everywhere, and must be kept off and driven out by a solid instruction constantly repeated and kept alive. Let us not forget Döllinger's golden words (*Kirche und Kirchen*, p. xxxi.): "Also this we have to acknowledge, that in the Church the rust of abuses and of superstitious mechanism always gathers again; that the ministers of the Church sometimes by their supineness and imprudence, and the people by their ignorance, materialise the spiritual element in religion, and thus lower, disfigure, and turn it to their disadvantage. *Therefore the right reformatory spirit in the Church must never disappear*, but rather periodically burst forth with quickening vigour, and penetrate into the consciousness and will of the clergy."* This superstitious inclination is so strong, that even a man without religion falls a prey to it, as Disraeli in the Sheldonian Theatre (25th November 1864) truly remarked: "Man is a being born to believe, and if you do not come forward—if no Church comes forward, with all its title-deeds of truth sustained by the tradition of sacred ages and the convictions of countless generations, to guide him, *he will find*

* "Auch das haben wir anzuerkennen, dass sich in der Kirche der Rost der Missbräuche, des abergläubischen Mechanismus, immer wieder ansetzt, dass die Diener der Kirche zuweilen durch Trägheit und Unverstand, das Volk durch Unwissenheit, das Geistige in der Religion vergröbern und dadurch erniedrigen, entstellen, zum eigenen Schaden anwenden. *Der rechte reformatorische Geist darf also in der Kirche nie entschwinden*, muss vielmehr periodisch mit neu verjüngender Kraft hervorbrechen, und in das Bewusstsein und den Willen des Klerus eindringen."

altars and idols in his own heart and his own imagination." It is the duty of the priests and teachers to prevent the sound doctrine from being corrupted by superstition. Alas! how many of them have neglected and are neglecting their duty, and have thereby not only brought disgrace on our Church, but have jeopardised the souls committed to their care! But should we abolish the images because they *can* be misused? Then let us likewise discard the knife, the axe, the rope. Or would it not be better to instruct the people than to deprive them of an effective help and incentive to piety? (Cf. *Confessio Orthodoxa*, part iii. quæst. 56).

As to the *Relics*, and particularly the bodies of departed saints, they are more than images. The body, once a temple of the Holy Ghost, baptized, confirmed, fed with Christ's flesh and blood, waiting for a glorious resurrection in order to be united again with the soul—such a body is not mere dust, as you pick it up from under your feet. No; the personal union of the body and the Christian soul has left its indelible mark on these bones and ashes—a mark visible to faith, a mark of glory and holy awe. If already in the Old Testament (2 Kings xiii. 21) a dead body cast into the sepulchre of Elisha, when it "*touched the bones of Elisha revived and stood up on his feet,*" can we wonder that the bodies of New Testament saints were equally privileged? We read in the "Lives of the Saints" of many miracles wrought by their relics. The sages of our age sneer at the credulity of those people who believe in such "fables;" but would it not be more consistent to begin by doubting the reports of the Bible? Shall we not discard the "very inconvenient" nineteenth chapter of the Acts of the Apostles, where we read that miracles were wrought by St. Paul's handkerchiefs and aprons? Was not a simple act of faith sufficient? And when the woman who had an issue of blood touched the hem of the garment of Jesus, why did He not simply say, "Thy faith hath made thee whole," but *felt* a (healing) power (δύναμιν) issuing from Him? * Here

* The Syriac Peshito and Cureton's St. Luke viii. 46 have: "I perceive *dchailâ nfaq men(i).*" *Chailâ* is the Latin *robur*, power, strength. The Armenian translator gives it appropriately by "*zoruthiun,*" implying bodily energy and efficacy.

was clearly not only a spiritual but also a bodily action at work. The Rationalists at the beginning of our century used to explain all these miracles by their pet theory, that Jesus and the Apostles stooped down and *accommodated* themselves to the prejudices and superstitions of their time. At present, inspiration having been minimised or exploded altogether by our Rationalists, an explanation of such difficulties is no longer needed—the believers are simply derided. We of the old stock cling to the traditional teaching agreeing with the scriptural proofs. A continuous string of testimonies from the Fathers can be found in every good dogmatical text-book. It is superfluous to remark that *only genuine and well-authenticated* relics can claim our veneration. The Church does not compel us to accept on trust any relic, but leaves us perfectly unfettered in our judgment.

If we go to the very bottom of the question why the Anglican Church (and the Protestant Church generally) has done away with the use of relics and images, and why they could not even make use of them if they wished to reintroduce them, we find the real reason in the abolition of the doctrine of the *invocation of saints and angels.* This doctrine furnishes the key to that of the veneration of relics and images, and is itself an integral part of the doctrine of the *Communion of Saints,* which the Anglicans, together with all the other Protestants, have retained only in a mangled and distorted condition. This doctrine, in its true and Orthodox form, is not only fraught with the greatest consolations and blessings, but radiates, as it were, into all the other doctrines of our religion, showing that marvellous bond of unity between the single doctrines, linked inseparably together, unintelligible if disjointed, subversive of each other if even a single one is denied or distorted, but shining in sublime harmony if Orthodoxy is preserved intact.

In the beginning of this treatise we have shown that *the Church* has two sides or aspects implied in her very name, viz., (1.) *ecclesia, i.e.,* a body vested with *authority;* and (2.) *kyriake, i.e., the household of God and family of Christ.* Hitherto we have chiefly dwelt on considering the first side. Now we must view the second side. Fifteen years ago we did this in our book "*Catholic Orthodoxy and Anglo-Catholicism*" (London: Trübner, 1866), and we need only reproduce what we have said there, inserting some few additions.

The Church is the *Body of Christ* (Eph. i. 23), and "we are members of His body, of His flesh and of His bones" (Eph. v. 30). Christ is the true Vine, and we are its branches. But this union is not to be understood of a hidden and invisible Church, for "every branch in me that beareth not fruit He taketh away" (St. John xv. 2). Hence the withered branch was also a branch, and consequently the Church, which is spoken of as the body of Christ, is *the visible Church*, whose members are incorporated in Christ by baptism, and bound to believe His doctrine, and to observe His commandments. This body of Christ is mystically but *really* (not only figuratively) animated by Christ's Spirit (hence the Church's *Infallibility*), pervaded by His own sacramental powers, defended by His Almighty arm. Christ is her Head, her only Head (which needs not the paltry representation by a Vicar on earth); she feeds upon Christ; in her veins circulates Christ's blood. Such an aspect of the Church as *Christ's living organism* must show at once how the poor miserable idea of a Zwinglian or Calvinistic Lord's Supper could scarcely find an understanding with the Catholics, who require infinitely more for the support of their life in the Church. Even Luther's Christified Bread or Impanate Christ was sure to be exploded by the Church as a kind of Eucharistic Monophysitism.

The Church is *tripartite*, the "Ecclesia Militans" on earth, the "Ecclesia Triumphans" of the departed saints, and the "Ecclesia Laborans" of those who "have departed with faith, but without having had time to bring forth fruits worthy of repentance. St. Basil the Great in his prayers for Pentecost says that the Lord vouchsafes to receive from us propitiatory prayers and sacrifices *for those that are kept in Hades*, and allows us the hope of obtaining for them peace, relief, and freedom." (The longer Russian Catechism on the eleventh article of the Creed.)

This *triune* Church is INSEPARABLY LINKED BY A SOLIDARITY OF INTERESTS, so that if "one member suffer, all the members suffer with it, or one member be honoured, all the members rejoice with it." "That there should be no schism in the body, but that the members should have the same care one for another" (1 Cor. xii. 26, 25). Such is the wonderful, mysterious vitality of the Church *in* Christ* and *through* Christ, that even the gates of hell cannot prevail against her. Such is her *Penetrancy*, that neither Heaven nor Hades can form a wall of partition. Only between the Church and hell (where the damned souls, the withered branches, are finally gathered) "there is a great gulf fixed, so that they which would pass from hence to you cannot, neither can they pass to us that would come from thence" (St. Luke xvi. 26).

This is the substance of the doctrine of the "Communion of Saints," a doctrine the bearing of which is boundless, by far exceeding the reach of human thought; a doctrine so comprehensive, so consolatory, so encouraging to Christian energy, and at the same time instilling the deepest humility, that every true Catholic must feel most deeply indebted to the Lord for this His inestimable benefit, so much the more so, as the Protestants have rent the Church which Christ knitted together by an indissoluble bond, have broken the intercourse between the two worlds, and confined themselves to the poor help which the sinful pilgims here below bring one to another. They say: "God is our only help; Christ is our only Mediator; we need nobody else." But whoever doubted the truism you advance? Or do you doubt it yourselves, perhaps, because you ask your brother to pray for you and with you? Or cannot God Himself help mankind, since He sends His angels to minister to them? Is it not an unjustifiable mistake of Christ, when speaking of the offence of despising the little ones, to point to the angels, saying: "Take heed that ye despise not one of these little ones; for I say unto you, that in heaven their angels do always behold the face of my Father which is in heaven" (St. Matt. xviii. 10). Ought Christ not rather to have said: "Fear God's anger?" And how can the angels see

* Remark the pregnancy of the expression *ἐν Χριστῷ* (where you would expect *εἰς Χριστόν*), which superficial commentators interpret as Hellenism instead of *εἰς*; *e.g.*, 1 Cor. xv. 19; *ἠλπικότες ἐσμὲν ἐν Χριστῷ*—the hope arising from the incorporation in Christ.

or know our offences while they behold always the face of their Heavenly Father? Are they perhaps omniscient or omnipresent? I expect you will answer to the effect: "The angels will know the offences through God anyhow." Now it is the same answer I give you with regard to the saints. *How* they hear our prayers and supplications, our thanksgivings and praises, we do not know, but they will hear them through God anyhow. But a more serious question is started: "Why do you invoke the saints at all? Is it not sufficient to pray to God and Christ? Nay, is it not derogatory to His supreme honour to seek a secondary help, as if He was either too austere a master, or changeable and more accessible to clever advocates?" My friend, you are sentenced by your own words, since you ask your brother here below to pray for you and with you. Or is the invocation of saints wrong because the saints have cast off sinfulness, whereas the Scripture allows you to ask the intercession of sinful men? St. Jerome (*Adv. Vigilant.* tom. iv. p. ii. p. 285, ed. Martianay) says: "If the Apostles and martyrs, while still bodily alive, can pray for others, when they have still to take care for themselves, how much more [can they do so] after having obtained their crowns and after having gained their victories and triumphs?" * But *the original cause and principal reason* of the Invocation of Saints is unknown to you, as you are ignorant of the true notion of both the Church and the Communion of Saints.

This chief reason is the *Solidarity* (alluded to above), which engages the individual members of the Church to each other, so that they may not and cannot be unconcerned at any loss or gain, joy or sorrow, activity or sloth, of any member. If "one member suffer, all the members suffer with it," &c. "Likewise joy shall be in heaven over one sinner that repenteth more than over ninety and nine just persons which need no repentance" (St. Luke xv. 7).†

* "Si apostoli et martyres adhuc in corpore constituti possunt orare pro cæteris, quando pro se adhuc debent esse solliciti, quanto magis post coronas, victorias et triumphos!"

† You see they are better informed in heaven about our spiritual affairs than we may fancy. Protestantism is awfully anxious to keep heaven at a distance, and to deprecate its intermeddling with our affairs; but it is of no use denying or ignoring a bond which *de facto* exists, although you decline to reap its fruits and to avail yourselves of its blessings.

This mutual engagement obliges the Church to work on towards the attainment of her great end, viz., God's glory and honour, that He may be all in all. The pilgrims here below assist each other on their way home. The saints above, although personally safe, having reached their happy home, *do not, by merely changing places, discontinue their being partners in the Church work.* They encourage and push on the traveller by word and example, which they left behind them on their departure. They intercede incessantly for the success of the travellers, pleading before the throne of God as a friend does in the case of his friend. Meanwhile we "Viatores debiles et lassi" stretch out our hands to the heavenly regions, where good wishes for our welfare are entertained, and prayers offered up by our friends and associates. However, both the "Viatores" here below and the "Victores" there above feel a common sympathy for their faithful companions detained in the prison of Hades, both joining their efforts to release them.* Thus the Church work goes on briskly below and above, every member co-operating with the others, on the grand plan which Christ, the Head of the members, laid down to God's honour and our eternal bliss. Thus this great *Co-operative Society* prospers *in* Christ, *with* Christ, and *through* Christ. Now how is it possible to speak of dishonouring Christ by invoking His saints? Does not the whole turn on Christ, as the body on the soul, as the accidents on the substance? Is the Church not both χριστοφόρος (bearing Christ) and χριστόφορος (borne by Christ)? On the contrary, they dishonour Christ who deny this *co-operative* character of Christ's Church. In fact, they quite misapprehend this efficacious union of the triune Church, where no sound member ever dies or is severed from the others, no sound member remains solitary or destitute. Giving they receive, and receiving they give. Here you have the genuine type of Divine Socialism, aped and caricatured in the modern Phalanstères. Saint-Simon's reveries are but the abuse of a deep truth, and Lamennais trans-

---

* St. Augustine (*In Joan.* lxxxiv. in *Patrol. Curs. Compl.* tom. xxv. p. 1847) says: "At the Lord's table we commemorate the holy martyrs, not in order to pray for them, *as for others who rest in peace,* but that *they may pray for us.*"

ferred the qualities of the Catholic Church to the people universally.

The "Confessio Orthodoxa," p. 300 *seq.*, says: * "We implore the *mediation* of the Saints with God, that they may intercede for us. . . . And we *need* their help, not as if they assisted us by their own power, but that they may apply in our behalf for grace of God through their prayers. . . . *Yea, if we despise the mediation of the saints, we most grievously irritate the Divine Majesty*, not honouring those who unblamably served it (*i.e.*, the Divine Majesty)." Moreover I refer to the acts of the Synodus Hierosolymitana, chiefly the 8th Decree (Ὅρος) of Dositheus, Patriarch of Jerusalem, and to the 17th chapter of the Confession of Metrophanes Critopulos. Remark in this Orthodox teaching the unequivocal decidedness and precision of language. What a gratifying contrast with the tame style and subdued voice of the Romish teaching in the Council of Trent, which seems to be made for entrapping converts, presenting the *minimum* and hiding the *maximum*. Let our course be the contrary, laying before the reader *the strongest language* of the Orthodox formularies, representing the practical working of the system. Can you heartily adopt this mode of thinking and living? If so, it is all right. If not, do not think of joining the Orthodox Catholic Church.

Why should we always expressly repeat that the *mediation* † of the saints is only a secondary one? We think every one knows that by himself. St. Augustine *owes his eternal salvation* to his mother Monica, since she was the chief instrument by which God operated on him. God *can and does* operate without intervening medium, as the case of St. Paul's conversion shows. But *the rule* is that God operates and dispenses His grace through the medium of His saints. The reason is obvious as soon as you have well un-

---

* "Ἐπικαλούμεθα τὴν μεσιτείαν τῶν ἁγίων πρὸς θεόν, διὰ νὰ παρακαλοῦσι δι' ἡμᾶς. . . . Καὶ χρειαζόμεθα τὴν βοήθειάν τους, ὄχι ὡς ἂν νὰ μᾶς ἐβοηθοῦσαν ἐκεῖνοι ἀπὸ τὴν ἐδικήν τους δύναμιν· μά, διατὶ ζητοῦσιν εἰς ἡμᾶς τὴν χάριν τοῦ Θεοῦ μὲ ταῖς πρεσβείαις τους . . . p. 304: Μάλιστα ἂν καταφρονήσωμεν τὴν μεσιτείαν τῶν ἁγίων, παροξύνομεν τὰ μέγιστα τὴν θείαν μεγαλειότητα, δὲν τιμῶντες τοὺς εἰλικρινῶς δουλεύσαντας αὐτῇ."

† See our Addresses to the Western Orthodox: "The Holy Virgin Mary our Mother and Mediatrix" (*Orth. Cath. Rev.* vol. ix. pp. 55–63), and "The Church and the Communion of Saints" (*Orth. Cath. Rev.* vol. viii. pp. 68–77).

derstood and weighed *the living and working triune Church.* Jesus Christ founded His Church to be a living and efficient organism, which can only subsist by and through *mutual co-operation.* I showed above how deeply St. Paul understood and entered upon this vital characteristic of the Church. Now if the intercourse between the Triumphant and Militant Church were stopped, it would paralyse the whole organism; in fact, it would destroy the same. Look round yourselves; does God not operate upon us through our fellow-members of the Church? Does He not dispense His grace chiefly by their hands? And still His arm is not shortened; He needs no assistant in His work. But to kindle faith, hope, and charity in the body of His Church, He appoints the members of His Church to be the channels of His grace to each other, in order to *cement the Church,* which is the mystical body of Christ.

Here you have the full aspect of the sacred and sublime Church work, in which the Communion of Saints shows itself in its full brilliancy. No doubt you have often thought what may the Saints in heaven do? Now you see they do the same as we do, or rather that we ought to do, *i.e.*, labour in Christ's vineyard, in Christ's Church, help and assist us in our Church work. And we do the same, or at least we ought to do the same, that the Saints do in heaven; for heaven begins here on earth: "The kingdom of God is within you" (Luke xvii. 21), says Christ, and this kingdom of God is heaven. He who does not possess already heaven on earth will never possess it hereafter. This is the most comforting Orthodox view of the matter, which brings heaven down to this earth, and lifts our earth up to heaven, which pulls down the wall of partition between heaven and earth, which effaces the line of demarcation between life and death, which widens the range of our view far beyond this earth, and makes us live and walk on this earth in actual companionship with saints and angels. And why should we wonder at it, since we live here with Jesus Christ in the most intimate companionship; and where Jesus Christ is, there is heaven, there are all the saints and angels of heaven? Let us then no longer think of heaven as of a far remote country. Let us pray, let us pray *well*, just as Jesus Christ wishes us to pray, and directly Christ with all His saints and angels is with us as really as we are walking with our friends on earth, but more effectually, more profitably. All it wants is *faith*, a living faith, and practical Church-life: and you will *experience* the truth of the doctrines with a fuller certainty than any experimental science of this world can offer. You will not ask for miracles, because the wonderful design of God's providential dealing begins to dawn in your mind, and makes your whole life a continuous miracle of divine loving-kindness. Then you will understand the grand word of the disciple who was lying on Jesus' breast: "The *life* was the light of men." No truth can be fully understood but by living up to it. And no light can be imparted but by truth. But the truth, the full revealed truth, can only be found in Christ's One Holy Catholic and Apostolic Church, and this Church is our undefiled, unaltered, and unalterable Orthodox Church, for whose members Christ prays to His Father (St. John xvii. 17): "Sanctify them through Thy truth." Come then to the Church of Christ's truth and be sanctified!

"THUS SAITH THE LORD, STAND YE IN THE WAYS AND SEE, AND ASK FOR THE OLD PATHS, WHERE IS THE GOOD WAY, AND WALK THEREIN, AND YE SHALL FIND REST FOR YOUR SOULS" (Jer. vi. 16).